NEW YORK TEST PREP

Reading Skills Workbook

Literary Texts

Grade 3

ISBN 978-1692169268

TEST MASTER PRESS

www.testmasterpress.com

CONTENTS

INTRODUCTION
For Parents, Teachers, and Tutors

New York's English Language Arts Standards

Student learning and assessment in New York is based on the skills listed in the Next Generation Learning Standards. These revised standards were introduced in 2017 and replace the previous Common Core Learning Standards. The reading standards divide texts into literary and informational texts. This workbook focuses specifically on literary texts. It provides practice understanding, analyzing, and responding to a wide range of literary texts.

Understanding and Analyzing Literature

The state standards and the state tests both focus on using a broad range of challenging literary texts. This workbook provides practice with a wide variety of passage types. It includes common passage types like myths, fables, personal narratives, and poetry. It also includes more unique types like plays, legends, and historical fiction.

For all the passage types, students are expected to demonstrate in-depth understanding. Students need to use close reading to analyze texts carefully and to look at texts critically. Students need to understand what a text says, as well as recognize craft and structure. Students also need to evaluate texts, respond to texts, and make connections between texts. At the same time, there is a strong focus on using evidence to support answers. This workbook focuses on developing the advanced skills that students are expected to have, while giving students experience with a wide variety of passage types.

Developing Advanced Reading Skills

The question sets for each text require students to analyze texts closely and will encourage a deep understanding of texts. There is a strong focus on advanced skills like evaluating texts, making connections, and looking at texts critically. As well as answering multiple choice questions, students will develop their understanding by providing written answers, completing tables and diagrams, listing specific evidence from texts, and writing complete essays. These activities will ensure that students develop the advanced skills needed.

Preparing for the New York State English Language Arts Test

Students will be assessed each year by taking the New York State English Language Arts tests. On these tests, students read literary and informational passages and answer multiple-choice, short-response, and extended-response questions. This workbook will help students master these assessments. It will ensure that students have the ability to analyze and respond to all types of challenging texts, while having the strong skills needed to excel on the test.

Practice Set 1

Personal Narrative

Learning Guitar

Instructions

This set has one passage for you to read. The passage is followed by questions.

Read each question carefully. For each multiple choice question, fill in the circle for the correct answer. For other types of questions, follow the instructions given. Some of the questions require a written answer. Write your answer on the lines provided.

Learning Guitar
By James Kaufman

When my mom bought me a guitar, I was over the moon. My new guitar looked so cool. I wanted to pick it up and start playing straight away. Well, I did try. But it sounded like a dozen screaming mice! Screech! Eek! Eek! Twang! Oh boy, it was not as easy as I had imagined.

My music teacher began giving me guitar lessons for half an hour every afternoon. After my first lesson, my fingers were extremely sore. It was quite difficult to push down on the strings. Nylon-stringed guitars are a bit softer, so they don't hurt your fingers as much. My guitar has steel strings, so it was a bit hard at first.

After a few lessons and lots of practice, my fingers gradually became stronger. The muscles in my hands also became stronger. It took much more practice than just the half an hour lesson. I also had to practice on my own before and after school.

Then I started learning some chords. It took me ages just to play one chord. Then changing between chords took me even longer to master. My music teacher made it look easy, but it was tough work.

At home, I would spend 30 minutes every day practicing chords. Soon, I had learned quite a few and could change quickly between them. Then my music teacher and I worked on some strumming patterns. Strumming is when you move your hand up and down over all the strings. There are different patterns that you can follow. The strumming pattern is like the rhythm of the music. Achieving nice even sounding strokes is quite challenging.

Just recently, I began to learn about scales. Scales are collections of musical notes. Each pattern of notes has a different sound. There are so many scales to learn! Sometimes I wonder how I am going to remember everything! When it feels too much, my teacher reminds me that I only have to learn a little bit every day and it will soon all add up.

Learning an instrument can seem awfully difficult at first. The first year felt like climbing a steep mountain. It felt slow and difficult and like I was not getting far at all. But eventually I got to the top and realized just how far I had come. I looked back and was amazed at my progress. Learning has become easier, faster, and more enjoyable. It feels like running down the other side of the mountain!

Being able to play the guitar has been an enjoyable skill to have. Everywhere I go, I take my guitar. My family and friends love it when I play and sometimes they even sing along. It's especially good to take my guitar when we go camping. When we are sitting around the campfire, I get my guitar out and play.

If we practice hard and keep trying, we can become good at anything. Learning to play the guitar was harder than I thought and it was not always enjoyable. However, seeing my skills improve makes the hard work worth every moment. Now, I really enjoy the challenge of building on my skills and learning new songs. When I am able to play complete songs with ease, I will know that I have achieved my goal.

One day, playing the guitar will feel easy!

1   Read this sentence from the passage.

When my mom bought me a guitar, I was over the moon.

The phrase "over the moon" means that James was –

Ⓐ   very tired

Ⓑ   very happy

Ⓒ   very stressed

Ⓓ   very surprised

2   Read this sentence from the passage.

After my first lesson, my fingers were extremely sore.

Which word would best replace the phrase "extremely sore"?

Ⓐ   aching

Ⓑ   buzzing

Ⓒ   itching

Ⓓ   tickling

3   According to the passage, how are nylon strings different from steel strings?

Ⓐ   They cost less.

Ⓑ   They sound smoother.

Ⓒ   They feel softer.

Ⓓ   They last longer.

4   Based on the details in paragraph 3, list **two** reasons that playing the guitar became easier for James.

1: _____

_____

2: _____

_____

5   Which sentence from paragraph 5 best shows that James is improving?

Ⓐ   *At home, I would spend 30 minutes every day practicing chords.*

Ⓑ   *Soon, I had learned quite a few and could change quickly between them.*

Ⓒ   *Then my music teacher and I worked on some strumming patterns.*

Ⓓ   *Strumming is when you move your hand up and down over all the strings.*

6   Complete the diagram below by listing the **three** guitar skills that James learned in order from first to last. Write each skill listed below in the correct box.

chords   scales   strumming

	→	→

7   Read this sentence from the passage.

> **When it feels too much, my teacher reminds me that I only have to learn a little bit every day and it will soon all add up.**

What is the most likely reason the teacher tells James this?

Ⓐ   to calm him

Ⓑ   to challenge him

Ⓒ   to praise him

Ⓓ   to tease him

8   What does the photograph on the first page of the passage mainly represent James doing?

Ⓐ   having fun playing

Ⓑ   working hard and concentrating

Ⓒ   feeling annoyed and wanting to give up

Ⓓ   dreaming of a time when he can play easily

9   Which statement best describes a theme of the passage?

Ⓐ   Hard work pays off.

Ⓑ   Actions speak louder than words.

Ⓒ   Honesty is the best policy.

Ⓓ   Things are not always what they seem.

10   Which **two** words best describe James? Select the **two** best answers.

☐   brave   ☐   focused   ☐   kind

☐   determined   ☐   generous   ☐   loyal

☐   fair   ☐   humble   ☐   polite

11   In the first paragraph, the author describes his playing as sounding "like a dozen screaming mice." Why does the author include this simile?

_____

_____

_____

_____

_____

12   Why does the author compare learning the guitar to climbing a steep mountain? What does this description show about how it felt to learn the guitar? Explain your answer.

_____

_____

_____

_____

_____

13 Read this sentence from the second last paragraph.

Being able to play the guitar has been an enjoyable skill to have.

How does the author support this statement? Use **two** details from the passage in your answer.

_____

_____

_____

_____

_____

14 Which sentence from the last paragraph supports the idea that James has found learning to play the guitar rewarding? Select the **one** best answer.

☐ If we practice hard and keep trying, we can become good at anything.

☐ Learning to play the guitar was harder than I thought and it was not always enjoyable.

☐ However, seeing my skills improve makes the hard work worth every moment.

☐ Now, I really enjoy the challenge of building on my skills and learning new songs.

☐ When I am able to play complete songs with ease, I will know that I have achieved my goal.

15 How does James show that learning to play the guitar was difficult? Describe **three** difficulties he faced as he learned the guitar.

_____

_____

_____

_____

_____

_____

_____

_____

_____

_____

_____

_____

_____

_____

_____

_____

_____

_____

Practice Set 2

Myth

Donal and Conal

Instructions

This set has one passage for you to read. The passage is followed by questions.

Read each question carefully. For each multiple choice question, fill in the circle for the correct answer. For other types of questions, follow the instructions given. Some of the questions require a written answer. Write your answer on the lines provided.

Donal and Conal
Adapted from an Irish Folktale

Part 1

There was once in old Ireland a very fine lad by the name of Donal. He was not only a very fine lad, but a very cheerful lad. He would go for miles to a party or a wedding; and he was always welcome, for Donal knew where to wear his smile. He wore it on his face instead of keeping it in his pocket.

The dearest wish of Donal's heart no one knew but himself. His soul was full of music, and he longed to have a violin.

One night Donal was going home through a dark forest when a storm came up. He found an old hollow tree and got inside of it to keep dry. Soon he fell asleep.

After a while Donal was awakened by a strange noise. He peeped out, and he saw an odd sight. The storm had passed, and the moon was shining. Many elves were dancing to strange music played by an old, old elf.

Such strange dancing it was! Donal crept out of the tree and drew nearer and nearer.

Suddenly he laughed out loud and said, "Well, that's the worst dancing I have ever seen!"

The fairies were astonished and angry, and they all began to talk at the same time.

"We have a man among us!" cried one.

"Let us hang him!" cried another.

"Cut his head off!" cried a third.

But the queen stepped out among them and said, "Leave him to me."

Then she called Donal to her. Now Donal was a wee bit frightened, but he knew where to wear his smile, you remember. So he went up to the queen, smiling and bowing.

"You say our dancing is the worst you have ever seen," she said. "Now, show us that you can do better."

Donal smiled again and bowed low. Then he began to dance. Such dancing the elves had never seen! They clapped their hands and made him dance again and again. Finally, Donal was exhausted, and after making a low bow to the queen, sat down on the ground.

The fairies crowded around him.

"Give him our silver!" cried one.

"Make it gold!" cried another.

"Diamonds!" cried a third.

But the queen said, "Leave it to me."

She went up to the old, old elf who had been playing for the dance. Taking his violin from him, she gave it to Donal. You see, the queen knew the dearest wish of his heart.

Then Donal was a happy lad, indeed! He thanked the queen and went home playing on his new violin.

Part 2

There lived near Donal's home a lad named Conal. He was not such a fine lad as Donal, nor such a cheerful one. He was a greedy lad, and the dearest wish of his heart was to be rich. And he did not know where to wear his smile. If he had one, he kept it in his pocket.

When Conal heard what had happened to Donal, he wished to know all about it. So he went to him and said, "Donal, man, how did you get that beautiful violin?"

Donal told the story backward and forward, and forward and backward, from beginning to end, until Conal knew it by heart.

Then Conal said to himself, "I will go to the hollow tree and dance for the elves; but I shall not be so foolish as Donal. I will take their gold and silver, and their diamonds, too."

That night Conal went to the hollow tree and waited until the elves appeared. Then he crept out and watched them dance. And he said, just as Donal had, "Well, that's the worst dancing I have ever seen!"

The fairies were astonished and angry again, and again they all began to talk at once.

"Another man among us!" cried one.

"Let us hang him!" cried another.

"Cut off his head!" cried a third.

But the queen said, "Leave it to me."

Then she called Conal to her. Now Conal did not know where to wear his smile, you remember; he always kept it in his pocket. So he went up to the queen with a very sour face.

The queen said to him, as she had to Donal, "You say our dancing is the worst you have ever seen. Now, show us that you can do better."

Conal began to dance, and he could dance well. The elves were delighted. They clapped their hands and asked him to dance again, but he said roughly, "No, that is enough. Do you expect me to dance all night?"

The elves were silent then, and the queen's face was stern. But she was a just queen, and she said, "You have danced well. Will you have some of our silver?"

"Yes," said Conal, without a word of thanks; and he filled his coat pockets.

"Will you have gold?" asked the queen.

"Yes," said Conal greedily, as he filled the pockets in his trousers.

"Will you have some of our diamonds?" the queen asked, and her face was dark with anger.

"Yes, yes," cried Conal.

"You shall not have them, you greedy lad!" cried the queen; "you shall have nothing."

Just then a cloud passed across the moon, and the elves vanished.

"Oh, well," said Conal, "I have the gold and silver."

He plunged his hands into his pockets and lo! The gold and silver had turned to stones. Then Conal went home a sadder and a wiser lad.

1   What is the main idea of the first paragraph?

  Ⓐ Donal is a wealthy person.

  Ⓑ Donal loves travel and adventure.

  Ⓒ People think Donal is funny.

  Ⓓ People like spending time with Donal.

2   Which sentence from the passage reveals what Donal wants?

  Ⓐ *There was once in old Ireland a very fine lad by the name of Donal.*

  Ⓑ *He would go for miles to a party or a wedding; and he was always welcome, for Donal knew where to wear his smile.*

  Ⓒ *The dearest wish of Donal's heart no one knew but himself.*

  Ⓓ *His soul was full of music, and he longed to have a violin.*

3   Why does the queen give Donal the elf's violin?

  Ⓐ She knows it is what he wants the most.

  Ⓑ She wants him to sing and dance.

  Ⓒ She believes the silver, gold, and diamonds are too precious.

  Ⓓ She wants the old elf to stop playing the music.

4   Based on the illustration at the start of Part 2, which word would people most likely use to describe Conal?

  Ⓐ determined

  Ⓑ gloomy

  Ⓒ greedy

  Ⓓ unfriendly

5   Read the first paragraph of Part 2 below.

> **There lived near Donal's home a lad named Conal. He was not such a fine lad as Donal, nor such a cheerful one. He was a greedy lad, and the dearest wish of his heart was to be rich. And he did not know where to wear his smile. If he had one, he kept it in his pocket.**

Which statement best describes this paragraph?

Ⓐ   It tells a cause and effect.

Ⓑ   It compares and contrasts.

Ⓒ   It gives a problem and solution.

Ⓓ   It offers facts and opinions.

6   Read this sentence from the passage.

> **Donal told the story backward and forward, and forward and backward, from beginning to end, until Conal knew it by heart.**

The phrase "knew it by heart" means that Conal —

Ⓐ   was jealous of it

Ⓑ   loved Donal for it

Ⓒ   remembered it well

Ⓓ   care about it a lot

7   List **two** details that show that Conal is rude to the elves when he dances for them.

1: _____

_____

2: _____

_____

8   Which sentence from the passage shows that Conal is not grateful to the elves?

     Ⓐ   *"Yes," said Conal, without a word of thanks; and he filled his coat pockets.*

     Ⓑ   *"Yes," said Conal greedily, as he filled the pockets in his trousers.*

     Ⓒ   *"Yes, yes," cried Conal.*

     Ⓓ   *"Oh, well," said Conal, "I have the gold and silver."*

9   A main theme of the passage is about the importance of being –

     Ⓐ   honest and true

     Ⓑ   kind and thoughtful

     Ⓒ   positive and happy

     Ⓓ   clever and witty

10   How does Donal feel when he sees the elves dancing? Use **two** details from the passage to support your answer.

_____

_____

_____

_____

11   Complete the web below by listing **three** ways you can tell that the elves love Donal's dancing.

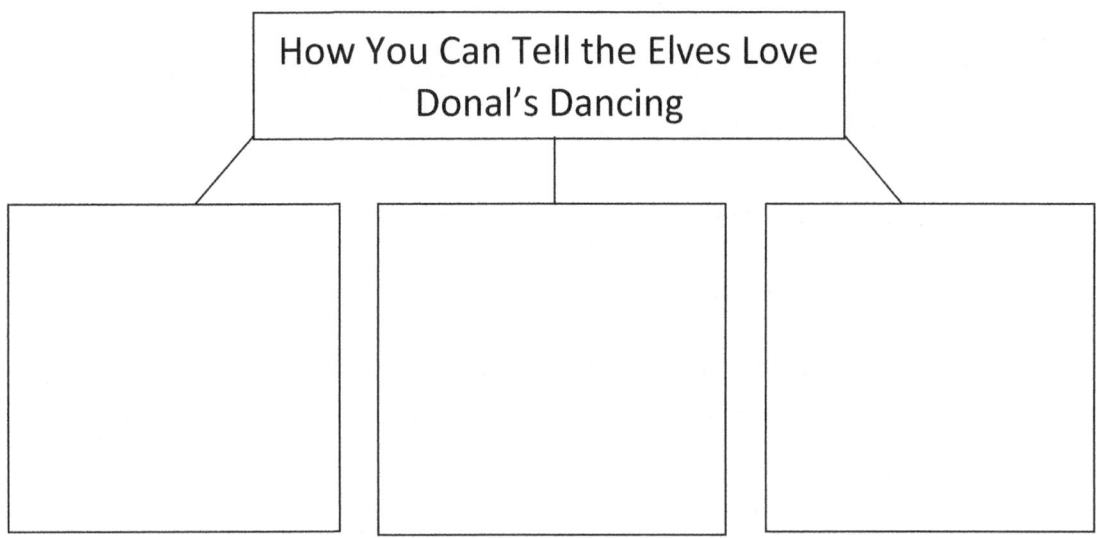

How You Can Tell the Elves Love Donal's Dancing

12   Compare how the elves feel about Donal before he dances with how they feel about him after he dances. Use **two** details from the passage to support your answer.

_____

_____

_____

_____

_____

13   Which phrase uses wording that fits the old Irish setting? Select the **one** best answer.

☐   "drew nearer and nearer"

☐   "wee bit frightened"

☐   "dearest wish of his heart"

☐   "very sour face"

☐   "dark with anger"

☐   "cloud passed across the moon"

☐   "plunged his hands into his pockets"

14   How does the queen punish Conal for being greedy? Use **two** details from the passage to support your answer.

_____

_____

_____

_____

_____

15 Why does the story have a happy ending for Donal but not Conal? Use **three** details from the passage to support your answer.

_____

_____

_____

_____

_____

_____

_____

_____

_____

_____

_____

_____

_____

_____

Practice Set 3

Play

The Vain Jackdaw

Instructions

This set has one passage for you to read. The passage is followed by questions.

Read each question carefully. For each multiple choice question, fill in the circle for the correct answer. For other types of questions, follow the instructions given. Some of the questions require a written answer. Write your answer on the lines provided.

The Vain Jackdaw

TIME: *last summer*
PLACE: *a public park*

[*The* JACKDAWS *are seen in the park.*]

OLD JACKDAW: Come, jackdaws! We must have our breakfast. Come!

[*The Vain Jackdaw stops to look at something on the ground.*]

OLD JACKDAW (*to Vain Jackdaw*): Come, no one should stop to look at anything! Come!

YOUNG JACKDAW: Just look at him. He takes up feathers!

VAIN JACKDAW (*to himself*): How fine I would look in these peacock feathers!

ANOTHER JACKDAW: See how he sticks the feathers in among his own!

YOUNG JACKDAW: See how he struts about in them!

OLD JACKDAW: My son, take off those feathers!

VAIN JACKDAW: It pleases me to wear them.

OLD JACKDAW: Take them off, I say!

VAIN JACKDAW: I will not take them off!

OLD JACKDAW: Then you cannot stay with us.

VAIN JACKDAW: I do not wish to stay with jackdaws. I will not walk with jackdaws. I will not talk with jackdaws. I think myself too fine for jackdaws.

OLD JACKDAW: Then, jackdaws, we will think no more about him. Come, now, to find our breakfast! Come!

[*They go. The* PEACOCKS *enter.*]

VAIN JACKDAW: Good morning, brothers.

PEACOCKS: Ha, ha, ha!

VAIN JACKDAW: Why do you laugh so, brothers?

PEACOCKS: Ha, ha, ha!

VAIN JACKDAW: You must not laugh, dear brothers. I am a peacock like yourselves.

FIRST PEACOCK: You silly jackdaw!

VAIN JACKDAW: I am no jackdaw. Do I not have feathers like your own?

SECOND PEACOCK: Ha, ha! I dropped them on the ground this morning.

THIRD PEACOCK: Let's take them from him!

VAIN JACKDAW: No, no! I beg you—

FIRST PEACOCK: Come, let's pull them out!

[*They pull the peacock feathers from the jackdaw.*]

THIRD PEACOCK: You cannot stay with us!

SECOND PEACOCK: Go back to the jackdaws!

FIRST PEACOCK: Away with you! Away!

[*The jackdaw runs. The peacocks go, laughing. The other* JACKDAWS *enter, followed by the* VAIN JACKDAW.]

VAIN JACKDAW: Ah, here you are! I have been looking for you.

OLD JACKDAW: Why do you look for us?

VAIN JACKDAW: I am a jackdaw. I want to be with jackdaws.

OLD JACKDAW: We will have nothing more to do with you! Away!

VAIN JACKDAW: But, brothers, my dear, dear brothers, please let me stay with you!

OLD JACKDAW: You would not walk with jackdaws! Away!

YOUNG JACKDAW: You would not talk with jackdaws! Away!

ANOTHER JACKDAW: You thought yourself too fine for jackdaws! Away!

ALL JACKDAWS: Away! Away!

[*They drive the Vain Jackdaw from the park.*]

1   Read the details below.

> **TIME:** *last summer*
> **PLACE:** *a public park*

Which of these do the details tell the reader?

Ⓐ   characters

Ⓑ   plot

Ⓒ   setting

Ⓓ   theme

2   Read this line from the play.

> **VAIN JACKDAW (*to himself*): How fine I would look in these peacock feathers!**

As it is used in the line, what does the word *fine* mean?

Ⓐ   beautiful

Ⓑ   shiny

Ⓒ   slim

Ⓓ   unique

3   At the beginning of the play, how does the author show that the vain jackdaw is picking up feathers and adding them to his own?

Ⓐ   The author describes the scene.

Ⓑ   Other jackdaws tell what is happening.

Ⓒ   The vain jackdaw gives his thoughts.

Ⓓ   The actions are described by an outside narrator.

4   One of the jackdaws describes how the vain jackdaw "struts about." The word *struts* suggests that he is —

ⓐ   showing off

ⓑ   feeling shy

ⓒ   moving quickly

ⓓ   walking unsteadily

5   Read this line from the play.

OLD JACKDAW: Take them off, I say!

How would the old jackdaw most likely sound when speaking?

ⓐ   amused

ⓑ   calm

ⓒ   stern

ⓓ   worried

6   Complete the web below by listing **three** things the vain jackdaw says he will not do with the jackdaws when he rejects them.

```
┌─────────────────────────────────┐
│   What the Vain Jackdaw Will Not │
│      Do with the Jackdaws        │
└─────────────────────────────────┘
```

┌────────────┐ ┌────────────┐ ┌────────────┐
│   │ │   │ │   │
│   │ │   │ │   │
└────────────┘ └────────────┘ └────────────┘

7 Based on the way the old jackdaw acts and talks, which word best describes his role in the group?

Ⓐ joker

Ⓑ leader

Ⓒ teacher

Ⓓ villain

8 Select the **two** lines that tell an action the peacocks will take.

☐ FIRST PEACOCK: You silly jackdaw!

☐ SECOND PEACOCK: Ha, ha! I dropped them on the ground this morning.

☐ THIRD PEACOCK: Let's take them from him!

☐ FIRST PEACOCK: Come, let's pull them out!

☐ THIRD PEACOCK: You cannot stay with us!

☐ SECOND PEACOCK: Go back to the jackdaws!

☐ FIRST PEACOCK: Away with you! Away!

9 How do the peacocks seem to feel about the vain jackdaw wearing their feathers?

Ⓐ amused by him

Ⓑ confused by him

Ⓒ curious about him

Ⓓ scared by him

10 List **two** details from the play that support your answer to Question 9.

1: _____

_____

2: _____

_____

11 Why does the vain jackdaw refer to the peacocks as "brothers"? What does this show about how he feels about the peacocks? Explain your answer.

_____

_____

_____

_____

_____

12 Do you think the illustration shows the vain jackdaw when he first meets the peacocks or after the peacocks have rejected him? Explain why you feel that way.

_____

_____

_____

_____

_____

13 Why does the vain jackdaw want to go back and join the other jackdaws at the end of the play? Use **two** details from the play to support your answer.

_____

_____

_____

_____

_____

14 Read these lines from the end of the play.

OLD JACKDAW: You would not walk with jackdaws! Away!

YOUNG JACKDAW: You would not talk with jackdaws! Away!

ANOTHER JACKDAW: You thought yourself too fine for jackdaws! Away!

Why do the jackdaws say these lines? In your answer, explain how they relate to earlier events in the play.

_____

_____

_____

_____

15   What lesson does the vain jackdaw learn in the play? Use **three** details from the play to support your answer.

_____

_____

_____

_____

_____

_____

_____

_____

_____

_____

_____

_____

_____

_____

_____

_____

Practice Set 4

Historical Fiction

Making History – Henry Ford

Instructions

This set has one passage for you to read. The passage is followed by questions.

Read each question carefully. For each multiple choice question, fill in the circle for the correct answer. For other types of questions, follow the instructions given. Some of the questions require a written answer. Write your answer on the lines provided.

Nina was asked to write a short story about a famous person. She researched the life of Henry Ford and imagined what it would be like to be him. She wrote this story about Henry Ford.

Making History – Henry Ford

I grew up on our family farm in Wayne County, Michigan. I did not like farm work at all. It meant long days in the sun, hard work, and smelly farm animals. From the early days, I realized that farming wasn't for me. Our farm was successful, but I wanted to do something different.

I'd always had an interest in machines. I remember the day my father gave me a magnificent pocket watch. It was beautiful in appearance and so well-made. But I was fascinated with how it worked. I decided to take it apart and have a look inside.

I was able to take the watch apart and reassemble it. I developed quite an interest in watches. I also became quite skilled at repairing people's timepieces. My neighbors would often get me to repair their watches and clocks for them. They were impressed by my skill and attention to detail.

When I left the farm at age 16, I decided to pursue my interest in machines. I got an apprenticeship at a shipbuilding yard. I learned how to use many tools. I learned fast and my bosses praised my skills. I worked a lot on steam engines and developed an interest in them. Like watches, I was amazed at how engines worked. All those small parts came together to make something very powerful and useful.

When I got the job at Edison Illuminating Company, I was so excited. This was a new challenge for me and I would learn many new things. My skill was noticed by many at my new job. After some time, I was promoted to chief engineer.

Most people did not know that, in my spare time, I was designing a gasoline powered horseless carriage. This piece of machinery was known as an automobile. At first, I thought I may have been crazy to try something like this. But I decided to push on anyway.

I built my first automobile in 1896. Then I presented my design in front of the famous inventor Thomas Edison! I was nervous, but confident that I had built something amazing. Thomas loved my creation. He told me to build a second model and try to improve on the first one.

I worked on many models and made many changes. The Ford Model T was finally produced. I was happy with the design. It was ready for release and for the world to see. I remember hoping that the public would like my new creation as much as I did. "I'm sure people will love it," I reassured myself.

And love it they did! I was amazed at the success of the Model T. I remember feeling so happy when the orders for my new automobile kept flooding in. So many orders came that we were unable to produce Model Ts quick enough!

That is when I decided to look at the manufacturing process and try to speed it up. There had to be a better way to get these automobiles built and out the door. I implemented some changes. I increased the size of the production plant. I decided to use a moving assembly line during the building process. These changes allowed my workers to make automobiles much faster.

Everyone was talking about the Model T. I'll never forget when my friends told me that half the cars being driven around America were Model Ts. By 1927, my company had produced some 15 million Model Ts! This motivated me to go back to the drawing board. "How could I improve on the Model T?" I wondered. I put a lot of thought into how I could increase the engine's power and improve the brakes.

That was some time back.

And now here it is... The Ford Model A. I'm really proud of this one. It looks so attractive and is built to last. Compared to the Model T, it runs smoother and has loads of new features.

People have been saying to me on the streets, "I can't wait to see your new automobile, Mr. Ford. I'll be lining up to buy one as soon as it comes to the showroom." Wow! That's a lot of pressure.

I feel so nervous. There it is, sitting all alone in the middle of the showroom. I turn the light on. The beams of light hit the smooth, shiny surface. The seats smell new and shine like a freshly polished pair of shoes.

I say to myself, "I better give it one last clean before everyone sets eyes on my latest creation." I grab a clean cloth from the storeroom. Slowly, I begin to wipe every little bit of dust from the automobile's surface. I can't help but admire its beauty. It has stunning white wheels. The headlights are sparkling and the glossy paintwork shines in the light.

I'm interrupted by a knock at the showroom side door. There is a man standing in the shadows. "Let's go Henry. Time to show it off." With that, the big roller door starts to open. The sunlight pours in. And so do the people! Hundreds of people have come to see the new Model A and to give it a test drive. I think we are going to have some buyers today.

1   Complete the web by listing **three** reasons that Henry Ford disliked farming.

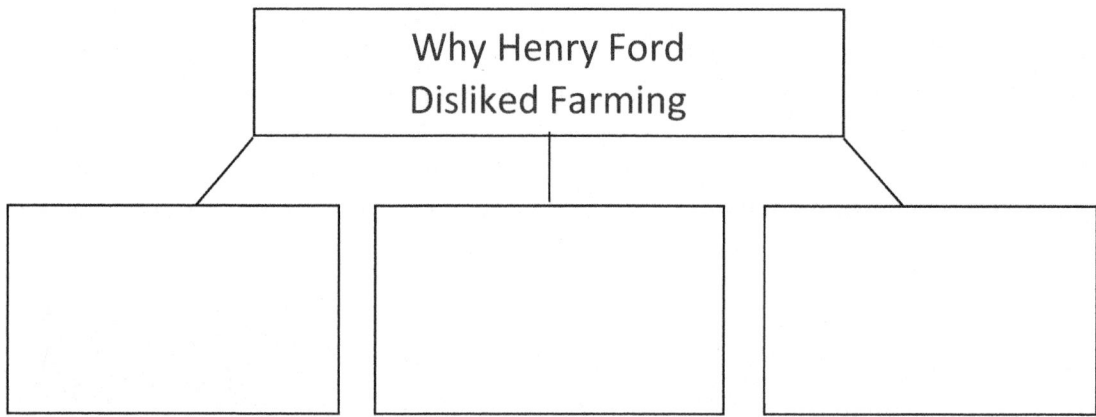

2   What most interested Henry Ford about the pocket watch his father gave him?

    Ⓐ   how well it was made

    Ⓑ   how it worked

    Ⓒ   how much it cost

    Ⓓ   how beautiful it looked

3   Read this sentence from the passage.

I was able to take the watch apart and reassemble it.

What does the word *reassemble* mean?

    Ⓐ   assemble again

    Ⓑ   assemble before

    Ⓒ   assemble better

    Ⓓ   assemble quickly

4   According to the passage, what was Henry Ford recognized for at both his jobs?

Ⓐ   his creativity

Ⓑ   his enthusiasm

Ⓒ   his leadership

Ⓓ   his skills

5   Read these sentences from the passage.

> **At first, I thought I may have been crazy to try something like this. But I decided to push on anyway.**

These sentences mainly suggest that Henry Ford is –

Ⓐ   willing to take risks

Ⓑ   scared of making mistakes

Ⓒ   curious about how things work

Ⓓ   keen to impress those around him

6   Thomas Edison tells Henry Ford to try to improve on his first model. Which sentence from paragraph 8 best shows that Henry Ford took this advice?

Ⓐ   *I worked on many models and made many changes.*

Ⓑ   *The Ford Model T was finally produced.*

Ⓒ   *I was happy with the design.*

Ⓓ   *It was ready for release and for the world to see.*

7   List **two** details from the passage that show that the Model T was a success.

1: _____

_____

2: _____

_____

8   Which phrase used to describe the Ford Model A best shows that it was high quality?

   Ⓐ   *looks so attractive*

   Ⓑ   *built to last*

   Ⓒ   *runs smoother*

   Ⓓ   *loads of new features*

9   What does the last sentence of the passage suggest about how Henry Ford feels when people enter to view the Ford Model A?

   Ⓐ   He is worried that people might damage it.

   Ⓑ   He is fearful that it is not as good as the Model T.

   Ⓒ   He is upset that he couldn't make it perfect.

   Ⓓ   He is confident that people will like it.

10 Nina has written the story as if she is Henry Ford. What would Nina most likely have had to imagine?

Ⓐ   where Ford grew up

Ⓑ   what Ford's first job was

Ⓒ   how Ford felt about the Model A

Ⓓ   the year that Ford built his first automobile

11 What did Henry Ford find similar about watches and engines? Use **two** details from the passage to support your answer.

_____

_____

_____

_____

_____

12 List **two** changes that Ford made to speed up the manufacturing of Model Ts.

1: _____

_____

2: _____

_____

13   The passage describes an automobile as "a gasoline powered horseless carriage." What does this description show that automobiles are replacing? Explain your answer.

_____

_____

_____

_____

_____

14   At the end of the passage, Henry Ford wipes down the Model A and admires its beauty. Complete the table by listing **three** physical features he describes to show its beauty.

The Beauty of the Ford Model A

Features
1)
2)
3)

15   How does the passage show that Henry Ford always wanted to make things better? Use **three** details from the passage in your answer.

_____

_____

_____

_____

_____

_____

_____

_____

_____

_____

_____

_____

_____

_____

Practice Set 5

Fables

Set of Two Fables

Instructions

This set has two passages for you to read. Each passage is followed by questions.

Read each question carefully. For each multiple choice question, fill in the circle for the correct answer. For other types of questions, follow the instructions given. Some of the questions require a written answer. Write your answer on the lines provided.

The Wolf and the Kid

There was once a little kid whose growing horns made him think he was a grown-up billy goat and able to take care of himself. So one evening when the flock started home from the pasture and his mother called, the kid paid no heed and kept right on nibbling the tender grass. A little later when he lifted his head, the flock was gone.

He was all alone. The sun was sinking. Long shadows came creeping over the ground. A chilly little wind came creeping with them making spooky noises in the grass. The kid shivered as he thought of the terrible wolf.

Then he started wildly over the field, bleating for his mother. But not half-way, near a clump of trees, there was the wolf!

The kid knew there was little hope for him.

"Please, Mr. Wolf," he said. His voice was trembling. "I know you are going to eat me. But first please pipe me a tune. I want to dance and be merry as long as I can."

The wolf liked the idea of a little music before eating, so he struck up a cheery tune and the kid leaped and frisked merrily.

Meanwhile, the flock was moving slowly homeward. In the still evening air, the wolf's piping carried far. The shepherd dogs pricked up their ears. They recognized the song the wolf sings before a feast, and in a moment they were racing back to the pasture. The wolf's song ended suddenly, and as he ran, with the dogs at his heels, he called himself a fool for turning piper to please a kid, when he should have stuck to his butcher's trade.

1   Read this sentence from the passage.

> **So one evening when the flock started home from the pasture and his mother called, the kid paid no heed and kept right on nibbling the tender grass.**

The phrase "paid no heed" shows that the kid –

Ⓐ   begged his mother

Ⓑ   fought with his mother

Ⓒ   ignored his mother

Ⓓ   misunderstood his mother

2   In the second paragraph, the author makes the scene seem scary. List **three** details the author includes to create this effect.

1: _____

2: _____

3: _____

3   The third paragraph describes how the kid "started wildly over the field, bleating for his mother." These details mainly suggest that he is –

Ⓐ   careless

Ⓑ   excited

Ⓒ   panicky

Ⓓ   sneaky

4   Select the **two** sentences that best show that the kid has given up and does not expect to escape from the wolf.

☐   The kid knew there was little hope for him.

☐   "Please, Mr. Wolf," he said.

☐   His voice was trembling.

☐   I know you are going to eat me.

☐   But first please pipe me a tune.

☐   I want to dance and be merry as long as I can.

5   Read this sentence from the passage.

In the still evening air, the wolf's piping carried far.

What does this sentence help the reader understand?

Ⓐ   why the dogs were worried about the singing

Ⓑ   how wonderful the sound of the singing was

Ⓒ   how the singing showed that the wolf was hungry

Ⓓ   why the dogs were able to hear the singing

6   When the kid speaks to the wolf in paragraph 5, his voice is trembling. What does this show about the kid?

Ⓐ   He feels afraid.

Ⓑ   He is very cold.

Ⓒ   He is trying not to laugh.

Ⓓ   He is tricking the wolf.

7   Read this sentence from the passage.

> **The wolf liked the idea of a little music before eating, so he struck up a cheery tune and the kid leaped and frisked merrily.**

How do the author's words help the reader imagine how the kid is dancing? In your answer, describe **two** words or phrases the author uses to describe the dancing.

_____

_____

_____

_____

8   How does the wolf's singing end up saving the kid? Use **two** details from the passage in your answer.

_____

_____

_____

_____

9 How does the wolf feel at the end of the passage? Why does he feel that way? Use **two** details from the passage to support your answer.

_____

_____

_____

_____

_____

10 Look at the photograph at the end of the passage. The photograph most likely represents the kid in which paragraph? Select the **one** best answer.

☐ Paragraph 1

☐ Paragraph 2

☐ Paragraph 3

☐ Paragraph 4

☐ Paragraph 5

☐ Paragraph 6

☐ Paragraph 7

The Miller, His Son, and the Donkey

One day, a long time ago, an old miller and his son were on their way to market with a donkey which they hoped to sell. They drove him very slowly, for they thought they would have a better chance to sell him if they kept him in good condition. As they walked along the highway some travelers laughed loudly at them.

"What foolishness," cried one, "to walk when they might as well ride. The most stupid of the three is not the one you would expect it to be."

The miller did not like to be laughed at, so he told his son to climb up and ride.

They had gone a little farther along the road, when three merchants passed by.

"What have we here?" they cried. "Respect old age, young man! Get down, and let the old man ride."

Though the miller was not tired, he made the boy get down and climbed up himself to ride.

At the next turnstile they overtook some women carrying market baskets loaded with vegetables and other things to sell.

"Look at the old fool," exclaimed one of them. "Perched on the donkey, while that poor boy has to walk."

The miller felt a bit vexed, but to be agreeable he told the boy to climb up behind him.

They had no sooner started out again than a loud shout went up from another company of people on the road.

"What a crime," cried one, "to load up a poor beast like that! They look more able to carry the poor creature, than he to carry them."

The miller and his son quickly scrambled down, and a short time later, the market place was thrown into an uproar as the two came along carrying the donkey slung from a pole. A great crowd of people ran out to get a closer look at the strange sight.

The donkey did not dislike being carried, but so many people came up to point at him and laugh and shout, that he began to kick and bray, and then, just as they were crossing a bridge, the ropes that held him gave way, and he tumbled into the river.

The poor miller now set out sadly for home. By trying to please everybody, he had pleased nobody, and lost his donkey besides.

1. According to the first paragraph, why do the miller and his son choose not to ride the donkey?

   Ⓐ   They are worried that people will be upset by it.

   Ⓑ   They do not know how to ride a donkey.

   Ⓒ   They want to keep the donkey in good condition.

   Ⓓ   They hope people will be able to see the donkey clearly.

2. Why do the merchants think the son should not be riding the donkey?

   Ⓐ   They worry the boy will fall off and hurt himself.

   Ⓑ   They believe that the elder father should be riding.

   Ⓒ   They think the donkey will move quicker without the load.

   Ⓓ   They fear the donkey cannot carry that much weight.

3. Read the paragraphs below that show the reaction of the people when they see the miller and his son riding the donkey.

   > **They had no sooner started out again than a loud shout went up from another company of people on the road.**
   >
   > **"What a crime," cried one, "to load up a poor beast like that! They look more able to carry the poor creature, than he to carry them."**

   List **two** details from the paragraphs that emphasize how upset the people are.

   1: _____

   _____

   2: _____

   _____

4   According to the second last paragraph, why did the donkey kick and bray?

　　Ⓐ　　He was uncomfortable being carried.

　　Ⓑ　　He did not want to be sold at the market.

　　Ⓒ　　He was trying to reach the river to take a drink.

　　Ⓓ　　He did not like the pointing, laughing, and shouting.

5   Read this statement made by one of the travelers in the second paragraph.

"The most stupid of the three is not the one you would expect it to be."

What does the traveler mean by this statement? Explain your answer.

_____

_____

_____

_____

6   Read these sentences from the passage.

Though the miller was not tired, he made the boy get down and climbed up himself to ride.

The miller felt a bit vexed, but to be agreeable he told the boy to climb up behind him.

These sentences show that the miller chooses his actions mainly to –

　　Ⓐ　　make other people happy

　　Ⓑ　　make his son happy

　　Ⓒ　　make the donkey happy

　　Ⓓ　　make himself happy

7   Why do the miller and his son carry the donkey into the market tied to the pole? Use **two** details from the passage to support your answer.

_____

_____

_____

_____

_____

8   Complete the diagram below to show the ways the miller and his son travel with the donkey from beginning to end.

How the Miller and His Son Travel with the Donkey

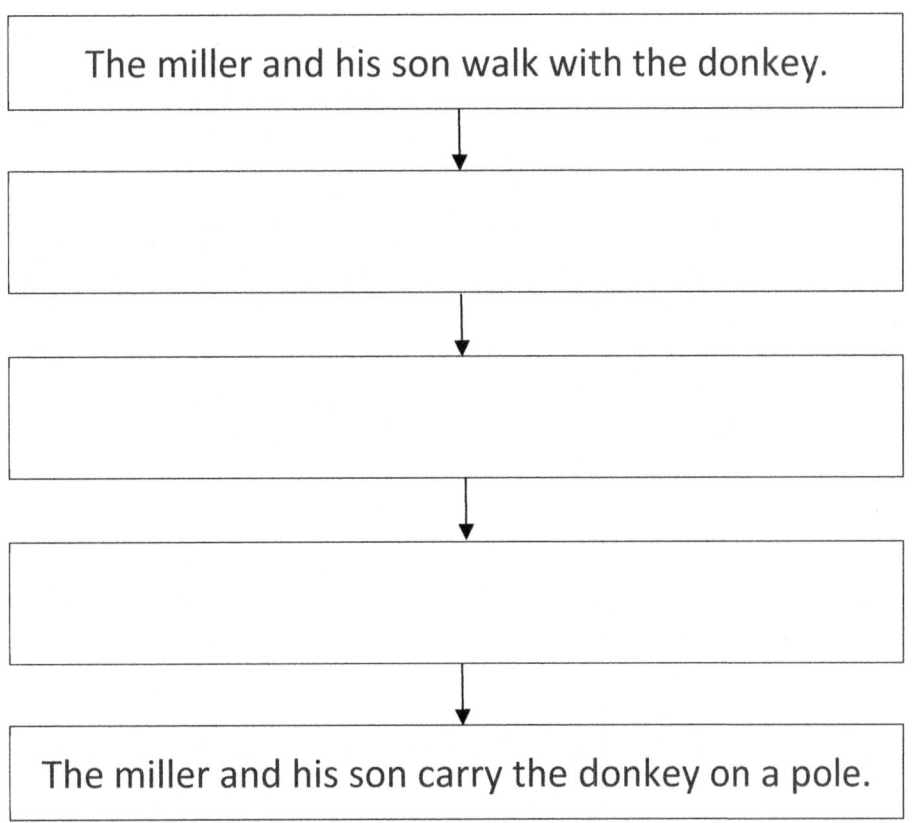

The miller and his son walk with the donkey.

The miller and his son carry the donkey on a pole.

9 According to the last paragraph, what is the message of the story? Explain your answer.

_____

_____

_____

_____

10 Based on your answer to Question 9, describe **one** way you could use the message in your own life.

_____

_____

_____

_____

Practice Set 6

Science Fiction

First Day on Mars

Instructions

This set has one passage for you to read. The passage is followed by questions.

Read each question carefully. For each multiple choice question, fill in the circle for the correct answer. For other types of questions, follow the instructions given. Some of the questions require a written answer. Write your answer on the lines provided.

First Day on Mars

"I don't want to!" Andy whined. Deni had to pull her brother by his arm into the airlock. She could tell he was scared, though she really didn't understand why. The airlock was only a small room, a passageway that allowed people inside the domes that covered the Mars colony to put on their spacesuits and go outside. During their six-month journey from Earth, they had all been told a million times that going outside was nothing to be worried about.

Deni sat her brother down on the small bench and shut the door leading back into the dome. Once they had their spacesuits on, the room would slowly drain out the dome's oxygen atmosphere and let in the Martian atmosphere. After just five minutes, they could open the outer door and go outside.

She lowered the helmet over Andy's head and secured the air-tight seal connecting it to his spacesuit.

Andy sat stiffly, gripping the edge of the bench with both hands, as if he expected Deni to try to pull him away at any moment.

"It's going to be fun! It's just like playing hide and seek on Earth."

"No it isn't!" Andy shook his head, almost in a panic, "On Earth, we don't have to wear THESE!" He pointed two thumbs at his own spacesuit.

Deni wanted to tell him he was being ridiculous, but figured it would be better to remain calm.

"It's just a spacesuit, Andy."

"You said it yourself! If it gets one TINY leak, then we're in HUGE trouble!"

"I didn't say you would get a leak. I was just explaining why we have to wear it."

"And what if I trip and crack my visor? There are rocks everywhere. I could easily fall on one."

"Your visor is far too strong to be cracked," Deni explained.

Andy still shook his head. "Why can't we just play inside, where we don't have to wear a spacesuit?"

"Mom and Dad didn't bring us all the way to Mars just to hide inside."

Andy looked out the airlock window at the reddish-brown landscape, "What if a dust storm comes?"

"There's no storm."

"But what if one comes really suddenly?"

"Then they'll tell us and we'll come inside. Now, come on! Everyone's waiting! See?" A dozen kids, all from their rocket, wrestled each other in their spacesuits. Everyone wanted to burn some energy after the long, cramped trip from Earth.

Andy crossed his arms defiantly. Deni reached over and flipped the switch on his chest that turned on his life-support system. Andy switched it off right away.

Deni turned it on again, "Remember how scared you were on Earth about getting on the rocket? That worked out okay, didn't it?"

"That was different." He reached for the life support switch one more time, but Deni gently pushed his hand away.

"Come on! It's going to be FUN!"

Through the visor on his helmet, Deni could see her brother was sulking.

"It's going to be fun," she repeated, "And every kid that was on the ship is playing."

Andy looked up at her, "I know."

"You don't want to be the only one left out, do you?"

He looked out the window at the other kids, finally admitting, "But I'm scared."

"I told you, it's safe."

"Not as safe as Earth."

"No, it's not as safe as Earth, but as long as you're careful about things, it's going to be fine. You have to be careful about things on Earth, too."

"Like what?"

"Like crossing the street. If you don't do it right, that can be dangerous, too. But you don't let it stop you from going to the park!"

One of the kids—Andy thought it might be his friend Darryl—had climbed onto a huge boulder and was waving back at him.

"If they can do it, you can do it," Deni told him.

Andy waved at Darryl.

"Did you know," she continued, "that you can kick a football three times as far on Mars?"

Andy turned to his sister, "No you can't!"

Deni rolled her eyes, "Then you probably don't know that you can also jump THREE times as high!"

Andy was suddenly interested, "Really?"

Deni nodded her head.

"Really. You know, things aren't as scary once you know the rules."

Andy thought about that for a moment, "Like crossing the street."

"Yes. And putting on your spacesuit the right way."

Andy considered that.

Suddenly, Andy leapt to his feet as if he wanted to try jumping right then. Deni quickly pushed him back down by his shoulders, "You'll hit the ceiling!"

Andy looked up at the ceiling, then broke out in a wide grin, "So, outside, I can jump as far as I want?"

Deni shrugged, "Pretty much."

Andy got up and stood by the airlock door, "What are we waiting for?"

1.   Which phrase from the first paragraph uses hyperbole? Select the **one** correct answer.

☐   "pull her brother by his arm"

☐   "airlock was only a small room"

☐   "domes that covered the Mars colony"

☐   "six-month journey from Earth"

☐   "all been told a million times"

☐   "nothing to be worried about"

2.   Which phrase best describes how the second paragraph is organized?

Ⓐ   order of events

Ⓑ   comparison of events

Ⓒ   cause and effect

Ⓓ   problem and solution

3.   Describe **two** ways the author shows that Andy is holding on tightly in paragraph 4.

1: _____

_____

2: _____

_____

4   Read this sentence from the passage.

> **Deni wanted to tell him he was being ridiculous, but figured it would be better to remain calm.**

Which word means about the same as *ridiculous*?

- Ⓐ   brave
- Ⓑ   embarrassing
- Ⓒ   silly
- Ⓓ   rude

5   Read these sentences spoken by Andy.

> **"You said it yourself! If it gets one TINY leak, then we're in HUGE trouble!"**

What is the most likely reasons the words "tiny" and "huge" are in capital letters?

- Ⓐ   They are words that Andy writes down.
- Ⓑ   They are words that Andy is repeating.
- Ⓒ   They are words that Andy is emphasizing.
- Ⓓ   They are words that Andy is whispering.

6   When Andy mentions a storm coming, Deni responds by saying that "they'll tell us and we'll come inside." This response helps show that Deni is –

- Ⓐ   kind and understanding
- Ⓑ   calm and logical
- Ⓒ   bold and adventurous
- Ⓓ   careless and rash

7   Which of these summarizes the main argument that Deni uses to try to convince Andy to go outside?

Ⓐ   He will have a lot of fun.

Ⓑ   He will make his parents proud.

Ⓒ   He will learn new skills.

Ⓓ   He will make new friends.

8   In which of these sentences is Deni encouraging Andy?

Ⓐ   *"I didn't say you would get a leak, I was just explaining why we have to wear it."*

Ⓑ   *"Mom and Dad didn't bring us all the way to Mars just to hide inside."*

Ⓒ   *"If they can do it, you can do it," Deni told him.*

Ⓓ   *Deni rolled her eyes, "Then you probably don't know that you can also jump THREE times as high!"*

9   In the passage, Andy is worried about things going wrong when he is outside the dome. Complete the web by listing **three** things that Andy says could go wrong.

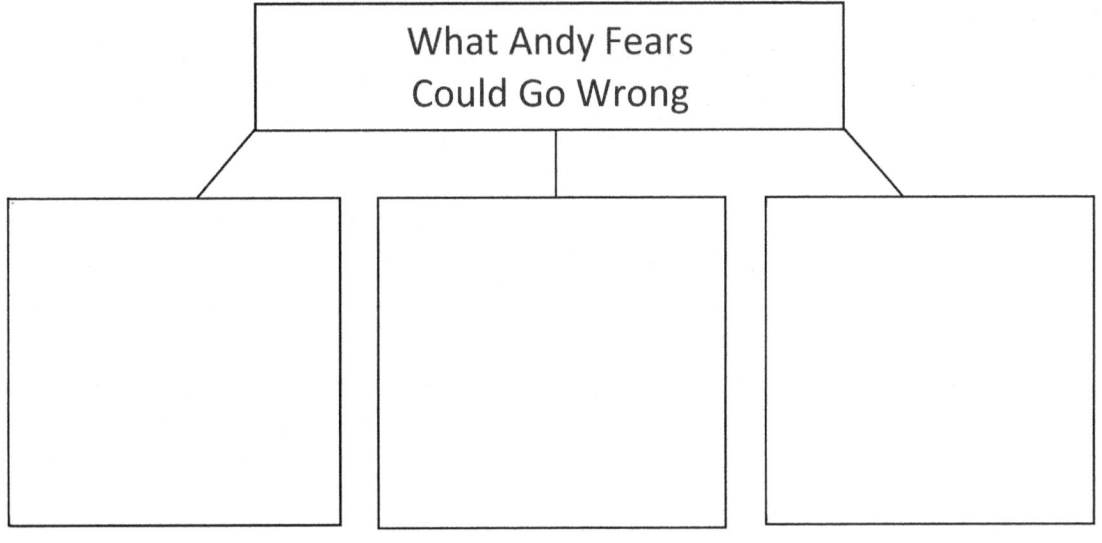

10   Which statement describes how the story is mainly told?

    Ⓐ   by a first-person description of events

    Ⓑ   by dialogue between characters

    Ⓒ   by a character revealing his thoughts

    Ⓓ   by a narrator recalling past events

11   In the passage, Deni mainly helps Andy –

    Ⓐ   learn patience

    Ⓑ   think of others

    Ⓒ   overcome a fear

    Ⓓ   stand up for himself

12   Based on the details in the first paragraph, describe the setting of the story. Use **two** details from the first paragraph in your answer.

_____

_____

_____

_____

_____

13 How do the details about kicking a football and jumping change how Andy feels? Use **two** details from the passage to support your answer.

_____

_____

_____

_____

_____

14 Why does Deni relate putting on a spacesuit on Mars to crossing the street on Earth? In what way are the two actions similar? Use **two** details from the passage to support your answer.

_____

_____

_____

_____

15 How does Andy feel at the beginning of the passage? How do his feelings change by the end of the passage? Use **three** details from the passage in your answer.

_____

_____

_____

_____

_____

_____

_____

_____

_____

_____

_____

_____

_____

_____

_____

_____

_____

Practice Set 7

Poetry

Set of Two Poems

Instructions

This set has two passages for you to read. Each passage is followed by questions.

Read each question carefully. For each multiple choice question, fill in the circle for the correct answer. For other types of questions, follow the instructions given. Some of the questions require a written answer. Write your answer on the lines provided.

A Busy Day

The bluff March wind set out from home
Before the peep of day,
But nobody seemed to be glad he had come,
And nobody asked him to stay.

Yet he dried up the snow-banks far and near,
And made the snow-clouds roll,
Huddled up in a heap, like driven sheep,
Way off to the cold North Pole.

He broke the ice on the river's back
And floated it down the tide,
And the wild ducks came with a loud "Quack,
quack,"
To play in the waters wide.

He snatched the hat off Johnny's head
And rolled it on and on,
And oh, what a merry chase it led
Little laughing and scampering John!

He swung the tree where the squirrel lay
Too late in its winter bed,
And he seemed to say in his jolly way,
"Wake up, little sleepy head!"

He dried the yard so that Rob and Ted
Could play at marbles there,
And he painted their cheeks a carmine red
With the greatest skill and care.

He shook all the clothes-lines, one by one,
What a busy time he had!
But nobody thanked him for all he had done;
Now wasn't that just too bad?

1   Read these lines from the poem.

> **The bluff March wind set out from home**
> **Before the peep of day,**

The phrase "before the peep of day" means that the wind left –

Ⓐ   early

Ⓑ   late

Ⓒ   quietly

Ⓓ   suddenly

2   According to the poem, how did the wind help the ducks?

Ⓐ   It dried their feathers so they could fly.

Ⓑ   It warmed the water so they could find food.

Ⓒ   It melted the ice so they could play in the water.

Ⓓ   It floated them farther down the river so they could find home.

3   Stanza 6 describes the wind waking a squirrel. The stanza mainly suggests that the wind is –

Ⓐ   mean

Ⓑ   playful

Ⓒ   sneaky

Ⓓ   strict

4   Which photograph shows a purpose of the wind that is NOT described in the poem?

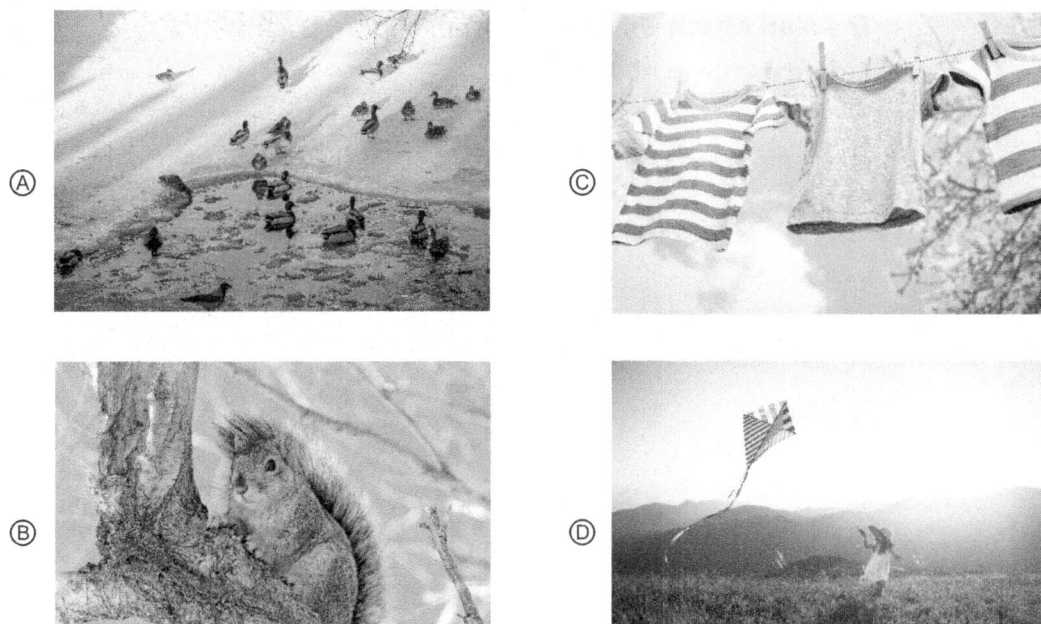

Ⓐ

Ⓒ

Ⓑ

Ⓓ

5   Which statement best summarizes what the poem described?

Ⓐ   why nobody cares about the wind

Ⓑ   all the positive things the wind does

Ⓒ   what it feels like to be the wind

Ⓓ   all the damage caused by the wind

6   Read these lines from the poem.

> **The bluff March wind set out from home**
> **Before the peep of day,**
> **But nobody seemed to be glad he had come,**
> **And nobody asked him to stay.**

Explain how these lines are an example of personification.

_____

_____

_____

_____

7   Read this line from the poem describing the snow-clouds.

> **Huddled up in a heap, like driven sheep,**

Describe the image of the snow-clouds created by this line.

_____

_____

_____

_____

8   Read these lines from the poem.

> **He snatched the hat off Johnny's head**
> **And rolled it on and on,**
> **And oh, what a merry chase it led**
> **Little laughing and scampering John!**

Describe **two** details the poet includes that makes the scene seem humorous.

1: _____

_____

2: _____

_____

9   If the poem was given another title, which title would best fit?

    Ⓐ   The Wicked Wind

    Ⓑ   The Wonderful Wind

    Ⓒ   The Whacky Wind

    Ⓓ   The Wild Wind

10   According to the poem, the wind is often –

    Ⓐ   hated

    Ⓑ   ignored

    Ⓒ   loved

    Ⓓ   misunderstood

Golden Keys

A bunch of golden keys is mine
To make each day with gladness shine.

"Good morning!" that's the golden key
That unlocks every door for me.

When evening comes, "Good night!" I say,
And close the door of each glad day.

When at the table "If you please"
I take from off my bunch of keys.

When friends give anything to me,
I'll use the little "Thank you" key.

"Excuse me," "Beg your pardon," too,
When by mistake some harm I do.

Or if unkindly harm I've given,
With "Forgive me" key I'll be forgiven.

On a golden ring these keys I'll bind,
This is its motto: "Be ye kind."

I'll often use each golden key,
And so a happy child I'll be.

1   Read this line from the poem.

To make each day with gladness shine.

This phrase refers to making each day –

Ⓐ   a useful one

Ⓑ   a happy one

Ⓒ   one that passes quickly

Ⓓ   one to remember

2   The poet uses an exclamation mark when describing how the speaker says "good morning" and "good night." The exclamation marks mainly suggest that she speaks –

Ⓐ   angrily

Ⓑ   excitedly

Ⓒ   kindly

Ⓓ   softly

3   Which term describes how the information in the last stanza is organized?

Ⓐ   by fact and opinion

Ⓑ   by cause and effect

Ⓒ   by problem and solution

Ⓓ   by compare and contrast

4   Draw a line to match each phrase below with a situation it might be used in.

Phrase

| Beg your pardon. |

| Forgive me. |

| If you please. |

| Thank you. |

Situation

| You want your brother to pass you the salt at dinner. |

| Your friend lends you a pen in class. |

| You bump into someone by accident. |

| You repeat some gossip you heard about someone. |

5   The main theme of the poem is about –

Ⓐ   forgiveness

Ⓑ   friendship

Ⓒ   happiness

Ⓓ   manners

6   Which of these does the reader of the poem mainly learn?

Ⓐ   how to behave well

Ⓑ   how best to start each day

Ⓒ   how to make friends

Ⓓ   how to cope with problems

7 Which technique is used in every stanza of the poem?

    Ⓐ   alliteration

    Ⓑ   personification

    Ⓒ   rhyme

    Ⓓ   simile

8 In the poem, the keys are a symbol. What do the keys represent? Explain your answer.

_____

_____

_____

_____

_____

9 The first illustration at the top is an example of how to react "when by mistake some harm I do." Describe the mistake that is shown in the illustration and how the girl is reacting to her mistake.

_____

_____

_____

_____

_____

10 Read these lines from the poem.

> **On a golden ring these keys I'll bind,**
> **This is its motto: "Be ye kind."**

What do these lines show about what all the "keys" have in common? Explain your answer.

_____

_____

_____

_____

_____

Practice Set 8

Nature Myths

Set of Two Myths

Instructions

This set has two passages for you to read. Each passage is followed by questions.

Read each question carefully. For each multiple choice question, fill in the circle for the correct answer. For other types of questions, follow the instructions given. Some of the questions require a written answer. Write your answer on the lines provided.

The Poplar Tree

Long ago the poplar used to hold out its branches like other trees. It tried to see how far it could spread them.

Once at sunset an old man came through the forest where the poplar trees lived. The trees were going to sleep, and it was growing dark.

The man held something under his cloak. It was a pot of gold—the very pot of gold that lies at the foot of the rainbow. He had stolen it and was looking for some place to hide it. A poplar tree stood by the path.

"This is the very place to hide my treasure," the man said. "The branches spread out straight, and the leaves are large and thick. How lucky that the trees are all asleep!"

He placed the pot of gold in the thick branches, and then ran quickly away.

The gold belonged to Iris, the beautiful maiden who had a rainbow bridge to the earth. The next morning Iris missed her precious pot. It always lay at the foot of the rainbow, but it was not there now.

Iris hurried away to tell her father, the great king of the gods Zeus, of her loss. He said that he would find the pot of gold for her.

He called a messenger, the swift-footed Mercury, and said, "Go quickly, and do not return until you have found the treasure."

Mercury went as fast as the wind down to the earth. He soon came to the forest and awakened the trees.

"Iris has lost her precious pot of gold that lies at the foot of the rainbow. Have any of you seen it?" he asked.

The trees were very sleepy, but all shook their heads.

"We have not seen it," they said.

"Hold up your branches," said Mercury. "I must see that the pot of gold is not hidden among them."

All of the trees held up their branches. The poplar that stood by the path was the first to hold up his. He was an honest tree and knew he had nothing to hide.

Down fell the pot of gold. How surprised the poplar tree was! He dropped his branches in shame. Then he held them high in the air.

"Forgive me," he said. "I do not know how it came to be there; but, hereafter, I shall always hold my branches up. Then everyone can see that I have nothing hidden."

Since then the branches have always grown straight up; and everyone knows that the poplar is an honest and upright tree.

1   Which phrase from the first paragraph shows that things have changed for the poplar tree?

  Ⓐ *Long ago the poplar used to*

  Ⓑ *hold out its branches like other trees*

  Ⓒ *It tried to see how far*

  Ⓓ *it could spread them*

2   Complete the table by listing the names of the three mythical characters who are part of the story.

Mythical Characters

Character	Role
	maiden
	king of the Gods
	messenger

3   Read this sentence from the passage.

The next morning Iris missed her precious pot.

What does the word *precious* tell about the pot?

  Ⓐ It is beautiful.

  Ⓑ It has special powers.

  Ⓒ It is usually hidden.

  Ⓓ It is important to Iris.

4   Read this sentence from the passage.

Mercury went as fast as the wind down to the earth.

Which literary technique is used in the sentence?

Ⓐ   alliteration

Ⓑ   metaphor

Ⓒ   personification

Ⓓ   simile

5   Which sentence best shows that the poplar tree is embarrassed when the pot of gold is found in its branches?

Ⓐ   *Down fell the pot of gold.*

Ⓑ   *How surprised the poplar tree was!*

Ⓒ   *He dropped his branches in shame.*

Ⓓ   *Then he held them high in the air.*

6   According to the passage, the poplar tree's branches grow straight up to show that the poplar tree –

Ⓐ   still feels sorry

Ⓑ   has nothing to hide

Ⓒ   cannot be trusted

Ⓓ   is never allowed to rest

7   Which phrase best describes the poplar tree's actions in the passage? Select the **one** best answer.

☐   a cruel trick

☐   a sneaky plan

☐   a serious error

☐   an honest mistake

☐   a careless blunder

8   What does the illustration at the end of the passage mainly help the reader understand?

Ⓐ   how long ago the events took place

Ⓑ   how poplar trees stick together

Ⓒ   how a poplar tree's branches grow

Ⓓ   how poplar trees are strong and proud

9   Read these sentences from the passage.

> **"Iris has lost her precious pot of gold that lies at the foot of the rainbow. Have any of you seen it?" he asked.**
>
> **The trees were very sleepy, but all shook their heads.**
>
> **"We have not seen it," they said.**

Are the trees lying to Mercury? Use **two** details from the passage to support your answer.

_____

_____

_____

_____

_____

10   Describe **two** features of the passage that show that the events described could not really happen.

1: _____

_____

2: _____

_____

Why the Parrot Repeats

In the olden times when the earth was young, all the birds knew the language of men and could talk with them. Everybody liked the parrot, because he always told things as they were, and they called him the bird that tells the truth.

This bird that always told the truth lived with a man who was a thief, and one night the man stole another man's ox and hid it.

When the other man came to look for it in the morning, he asked the thief, "Have you seen my ox?"

"No, I have not seen it," said the man.

"Is that the truth?" the owner asked.

"Yes, it is. I have not seen the ox," repeated the man.

"Ask the parrot," said one of the villagers. "He always tells the truth."

"Oh bird of truth," said they to the parrot, "did this man steal an ox and hide it?"

"Yes, he did," answered the parrot.

The thief knew well that the villagers would punish him the next day, if he could not make them think that the parrot did not always tell the truth.

"I have it," he said to himself at last. "I know what I can do."

When night came he put a great jar over the parrot. Then he poured water upon the jar and struck it many times with a tough piece of oak. This he did half the night. Then he went to bed and was soon fast asleep.

In the morning the men came to punish him.

"How do you know that I stole the ox?" he asked.

"Because the bird of truth says that you did," they answered.

"The bird of truth!" he cried. "That parrot is no bird of truth. He will not tell the truth even about what happened last night. Ask him if the moon was shining."

"Did the moon shine last night?" the men asked.

"No," answered the parrot. "There was no moon, for the rain fell, and there was a great storm in the heavens. I heard the thunder half the night."

"This bird has always told the truth before," said the villagers, "but there was no storm last night and the moon was bright. What shall we do to punish the parrot?"

"I think we will no longer let him live in our homes," answered the thief.

"Yes," said the others, "he must fly away to the forest, and even when there is a storm, he can no longer come to our homes, because we know now that he is a bird of a lying tongue."

So the parrot flew away sorrowfully into the lonely forest. He met a mockingbird and told him what had happened.

"Why did you not repeat men's words as I do?" asked the mockingbird. "Men always think their own words are good."

"But the man's words were not true," said the parrot.

"That is nothing," replied the mockingbird, laughing. "Say what they say, and they will think you are a wonderful bird."

"Yes, I see," said the parrot thoughtfully, "and I will never again be punished for telling the truth. I will only repeat the words of others."

1   According to the first paragraph, what was the parrot mainly known for being?

    Ⓐ   honest

    Ⓑ   intelligent

    Ⓒ   loyal

    Ⓓ   witty

2   Look at the photograph at the start of the passage. What do the parrots appear to be doing that relates to the first paragraph?

    Ⓐ   arguing with each other

    Ⓑ   copying each other

    Ⓒ   singing together

    Ⓓ   talking to each other

3   Read these sentences spoken by the thief.

    "I have it," he said to himself at last. "I know what I can do."

What do the thief's words reveal?

    Ⓐ   He is annoyed.

    Ⓑ   He has a plan.

    Ⓒ   He feels bad about stealing.

    Ⓓ   He knows where the ox is.

4   Complete the web below by listing the **two** other things the thief does to the parrot at night.

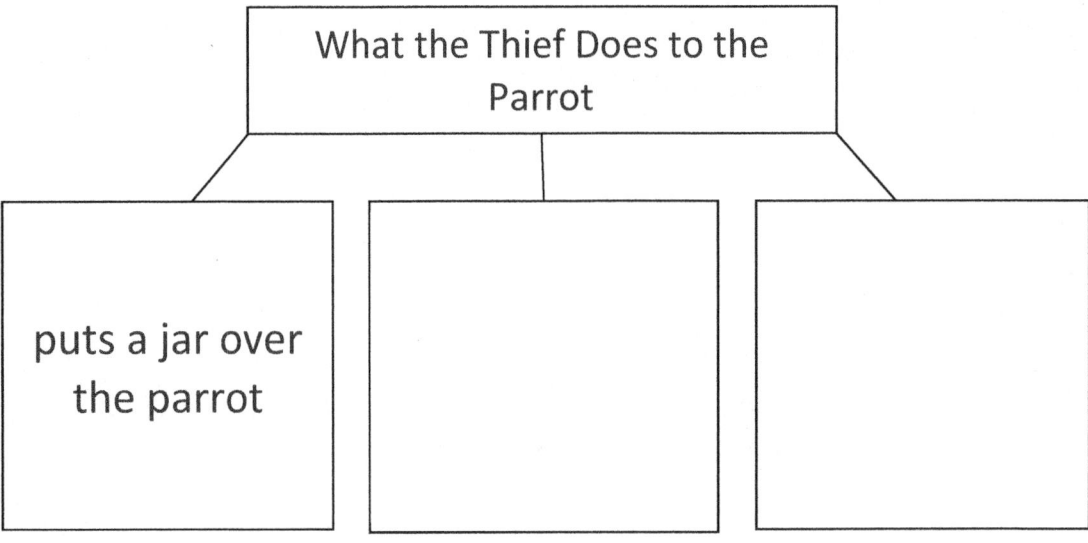

5   Based on your answer to Question 4, complete the list by adding the **two** other things the parrot thinks happened during the night.

1: <u>He thinks the moon was not shining.</u>

2: _____

3: _____

6   Which statement best explains why the parrot tells the villagers that there was a storm?

Ⓐ   He is confusing a dream he had with real life.

Ⓑ   He is trying to save his master.

Ⓒ   He has been tricked into thinking there was a storm.

Ⓓ   He is telling the truth because there was a storm.

7   Read this sentence from the passage.

So the parrot flew away sorrowfully into the lonely forest.

What does the word *sorrowfully* mean?

Ⓐ   angrily

Ⓑ   cleverly

Ⓒ   quickly

Ⓓ   sadly

8   What advice does the mockingbird give the parrot? Use **two** details from the passage in your answer.

_____

_____

_____

_____

_____

9 Read this sentence from the passage.

> **The thief knew well that the villagers would punish him the next day, if he could not make them think that the parrot did not always tell the truth.**

Does the thief's plan work? Use **two** details from the passage to support your answer.

_____

_____

_____

_____

_____

10 Describe **two** ways the parrot's relationship with people changes because of the events of the passage.

1: _____

_____

2: _____

_____

Practice Set 9

Adventure Story

Josie's Journey

Instructions

This set has one passage for you to read. The passage is followed by questions.

Read each question carefully. For each multiple choice question, fill in the circle for the correct answer. For other types of questions, follow the instructions given. Some of the questions require a written answer. Write your answer on the lines provided.

Josie's Journey

"Wake up, Miss Josie, wake up!"

Princess Josefina sat up in bed and rubbed her eyes. She was sure she had heard someone say her name. But when she looked around, no one was there. She was just about to go back to sleep when she heard it again.

This time she got out of bed. She noticed a shadow at the window. But it wasn't a shadow. It was a face! She almost screamed with fright. Then she saw it was old Monty who worked in the stables.

But what was he doing at her window? The castle was forty feet high, and Josie's room was right at the top. Her uncle said it was to keep her safe. But Josie knew the real reason was to stop her escaping. She wasn't sure what he thought she might want to escape from. Perhaps she was about to find out.

When she looked again she saw that Monty was holding on to a thick rope. The rope must have been attached to the roof above. As she opened the window Monty began to slide slowly down.

"Come on," he said. "We don't have much time."

Josie was standing in her nightdress and bare feet. She looked at the rope in horror.

"But, I..."

"It's okay, Missy. It's quite safe as long as you hold on. The old lady is waiting for us. She's got your clothes and things. Just grab what you need and climb on."

Josie walked over to the bedside table. She reached her hand down and pulled a small box from a hidden compartment at the back. Inside there was the necklace she had been given as a baby by the blind peddler. He had told her parents she would need it one day to keep her safe. As she pulled it over her head she wondered if that day had come.

Next, Josie scrambled onto the window ledge and reached out for the rope. She took a last look around her bedroom and hoped that someone would take good care of Samuel, the royal white parrot, still sound asleep in his cage.

Josie took a deep breath and clasped the rope. She swung her legs over and crossed them around the rope. Inch by inch, Josie eased her way down while always keeping her eyes straight ahead. She knew that you should never look down.

And all the time, she could hear Monty's voice.

"That's the way, Missy. Just keep going. Not far now."

They both breathed a sigh of relief when they reached the ground. And there was Nanny waiting for them. The old woman smiled even though she looked a little anxious. She carried a bundle of clothes wrapped up in an old checked blanket.

"Ah, you've got the necklace, I see. Good girl."

"Come on." said Monty. "There's no time to lose."

Nanny grabbed Josie's hand and they ran down the long driveway away from the castle.

"Quick! Left! Dive into the bushes," called Monty from ahead, where he had been acting as lookout.

All three took a sharp turn and jumped into the dark cover of the bushes. Josie hardly dared to breathe. She was so cold in her thin nightdress, she was afraid she would sneeze and give them all away. As she crouched in the bushes she could hear hooves getting closer.

From her hiding place, Josie could see the figures of the horsemen in the moonlight. She slowed her breathing and counted to fifteen. Finally, the hooves faded into the distance.

"It's your uncle's henchmen!" said Monty when they were able to speak again.

Once they were sure the danger had passed, they quickly followed Monty. He led them to the stables where Viola, Josie's young filly, was waiting. Josie started to put Viola's harness on but saw that Monty was taking Bronwyn, the chestnut mare instead.

"We'll need this old girl," said Monty as he got the horse ready. "Viola isn't strong enough for this, I'm afraid."

Meanwhile, Nanny was busy pulling things from the bundles she had been carrying. She passed the warm clothes to Josie who pulled them on over her nightdress. Last of all, she threw a green cloak over her shoulders. She was glad to feel warm again.

It was time to go. Before they left Josie turned to say goodbye to the filly. She stroked her nose.

"Don't worry, Viola. I will be back," she whispered.

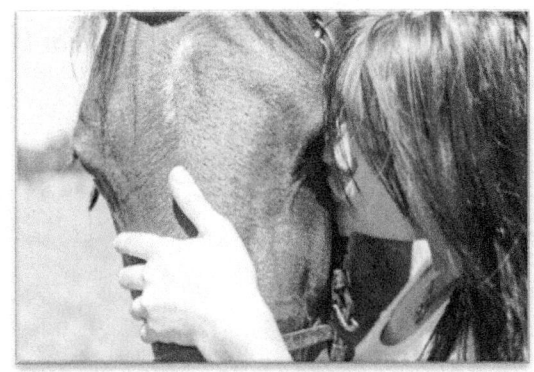

Then she rode off down the path just as the sun started to rise.

1   According to the passage, what wakes up Josie?

    Ⓐ   She has a bad dream.

    Ⓑ   She thinks she hears her name.

    Ⓒ   She sees a face at the window.

    Ⓓ   She spots a strange shadow.

2   How does Josie feel when she first sees the face at the window?

    Ⓐ   amused

    Ⓑ   confused

    Ⓒ   excited

    Ⓓ   startled

3   Which sentence from paragraph 4 best shows that people are lying to Josie?

    Ⓐ   *The castle was forty feet high, and Josie's room was right at the top.*

    Ⓑ   *Her uncle said it was to keep her safe.*

    Ⓒ   *But Josie knew the real reason was to stop her escaping.*

    Ⓓ   *She wasn't sure what he thought she might want to escape from.*

4   Which sentence spoken by Monty creates a sense of urgency?

Ⓐ   *"We don't have much time."*

Ⓑ   *"It's okay, Missy."*

Ⓒ   *"It's quite safe as long as you hold on."*

Ⓓ   *"She's got your clothes and things."*

5   Josie grabs a necklace before she leaves. Describe **two** details about the necklace that suggest that it is special and important.

1: _____

_____

2: _____

_____

6   Select the **two** phrases from paragraph 12 that show that Josie climbed down the rope slowly.

☐   took a deep breath   ☐   inch by inch

☐   clasped the rope   ☐   eased her way down

☐   swung her legs over   ☐   eyes straight ahead

☐   crossed them around the rope   ☐   never look down

7   Read these sentences spoken by Monty.

"That's the way, Missy. Just keep going. Not far now."

Which of these best describes what Monty is doing?

Ⓐ   hurrying Josie

Ⓑ   encouraging Josie

Ⓒ   scolding Josie

Ⓓ   warning Josie

8   Describe **two** details that show that Josie is tense as she waits in the bushes for the henchmen to pass.

1: _____

_____

2: _____

_____

9   Read this sentence from the passage.

All three took a sharp turn and jumped into the dark cover of the bushes.

As it is used in the sentence, what does *sharp* mean?

Ⓐ   clear

Ⓑ   clever

Ⓒ   pointed

Ⓓ   sudden

10   What does the photograph at the end of the passage suggest about Josie and her horse Viola?

　Ⓐ　Josie cares greatly about Viola.

　Ⓑ　Josie has had Viola since she was a young girl.

　Ⓒ　Josie fears she will never see Viola again.

　Ⓓ　Josie plans to take Viola with her.

11   Which word best describes the overall mood of the passage?

　Ⓐ　cheerful

　Ⓑ　exciting

　Ⓒ　gloomy

　Ⓓ　lonely

12   How does paragraph 4 emphasize how strange it is that someone would be at Josie's window? Use **two** details from the paragraph to support your answer.

　_____

　_____

　_____

　_____

　_____

13   Paragraph 7 states that Josie "looked at the rope in horror." Why do you think Josie reacts this way? Explain your answer.

_____

_____

_____

_____

_____

14   Why does Monty tell Josie to dive into the bushes? Use **two** details from the passage to support your answer.

_____

_____

_____

_____

15   How can you tell that Monty and Nanny are helping Josie escape? Use **three** details from the passage in your answer.

_____

_____

_____

_____

_____

_____

_____

_____

_____

_____

_____

_____

_____

_____

Practice Set 10

Mystery Story

Missing Shoes

Instructions

This set has one passage for you to read. The passage is followed by questions.

Read each question carefully. For each multiple choice question, fill in the circle for the correct answer. For other types of questions, follow the instructions given. Some of the questions require a written answer. Write your answer on the lines provided.

Missing Shoes

"Who would take them?"

The entire class crowded quietly at the back of the classroom, staring at the shelves where all of their shoes had been neatly lined up while they were across the hall taking dance lessons.

"*This* is why I don't like dance," Mark said.

To Celine, self-appointed Student Police Officer and Most Qualified Detective, Mark's statement was just as good as a confession. In fact, Celine looked at Ms. Teleson, expecting their teacher to escort Mark to the office right then and there.

The shoes were all on the shelves before the dance class, but where were they now?

But she didn't.

"Why are you looking at me?" Mark asked Celine.

"I think you know why."

Mark thought about that a moment, then looked down at where the shoes used to be, "You think I did this?"

"You have a motive."

"Yeah, but I wouldn't have said anything if I really did it!"

Celine thought he might have a point. Or, maybe he just wasn't smart enough to stay quiet.

"I didn't take the shoes, Celine."

"Innocent until proven guilty, Celine!" Mark's sister Erin jumped to his defense.

Maybe she was part of it, Celine considered.

Across the courtyard, she could hear the hooting and hollering echoing from the art classroom directly across from theirs.

Arthur, a short frizzy haired boy with huge glasses, made his way through the crowd to reach her.

"Who do you think did it?" he asked.

Celine looked down at the empty space where the shoes had been, and then noticed that Arthur's big toes were sticking out of his socks.

"You need new socks."

"If I had my shoes, it wouldn't matter."

"Do you have *suspects?*" Erin asked, hinting very clearly that Mark wasn't one of them.

The more Celine thought about it, the less she thought that he could be the culprit. As much as Mark said he hated dance, he'd been taking part the entire time. She had even danced with him.

"It can't be anyone in our class," she told Erin.

"It doesn't make sense," Mark added, no longer feeling accused.

Celine pondered the mystery, wondering what someone could possibly do with twenty pairs of shoes.

"Maybe it's a conspiracy," she wondered aloud.

"A what?" Arthur asked. Other kids gathered around her to find out what she meant.

"Maybe somebody in the class is working with someone outside the class. Maybe they worked *together* to take our shoes!"

"But *why?*" asked Marvin McKay, a boy who rarely said a word, but seemed especially irritated by his missing shoes, "*Why* would someone want to take our old shoes?"

"*My* shoes were brand new," Erin pointed out, "I could see why they would want to steal mine." She peered down at Marvin's bare feet, as if she could still see his shoes, "Yours, not so much."

"I don't think it has to do with the shoes," Celine suggested, "I think it has to do with us."

"Us? What did we do?" Mark seemed offended.

She couldn't blame him. It wasn't like gym class, where teams play against other teams, and people had rivalries. Even though their school was small, she hardly knew kids in other classes. They sort of kept to themselves. They could guess what other classes were studying by the ever-changing decorations they taped onto their windows.

Ms. Teleson liked to call them, "The Idea Windows," because kids in other classrooms could see and get inspired by the ideas of other kids.

Celine walked over to the big windows that faced out into the school's small courtyard and peered across at the other classrooms. On one set of windows, large cut-out drawings of animals decorated it, as well as letters spelling out "Mammals."

On their own window, at the moment, they had taped a display titled "Great Explorers." There were pictures of famous explorers, maps, and cut-out footprints that they had outlined from their own shoes! Could *that* have anything to do with it?

It was hard for Celine to understand what they were studying in the classroom straight across from them. There were swirls of paint and random images of people, animals, and even a dragon.

"What's going on over there?" she asked.

"Art class," Ms. Teleson replied. "I think they're making some kind of mobile today."

Suddenly, Celine's expression changed.

Without even asking Ms. Teleson, Celine marched out of the classroom. Everyone followed, including Ms. Teleson.

Celine marched through the halls, making a right and then another right until she was standing right in front of the door to the art class. From inside, she could hear a classroom full of kids laughing and seemingly having a good time. Without knocking, she pushed open the door. They all looked at Celine, in shock for a moment, and then continued laughing.

Celine finally understood: they had been inspired by Ms. Teleson's classroom. She looked up, and wasn't surprised at what she saw. A huge mobile hung from the ceiling, consisting entirely of shoes. Their shoes.

1   Who is the main character in the passage?

    Ⓐ   Celine

    Ⓑ   Erin

    Ⓒ   Mark

    Ⓓ   Ms. Teleson

2   Which change to the title would most help readers understand that it is a mystery story?

    Ⓐ   The Nicest Missing Shoes of All

    Ⓑ   The Magical Missing Shoes

    Ⓒ   The Missing Shoes Adventure

    Ⓓ   The Case of the Missing Shoes

3   What does the photograph and caption at the beginning of the passage most help readers understand?

    Ⓐ   what the main problem is

    Ⓑ   who the main suspect is

    Ⓒ   what the setting of the story is

    Ⓓ   why it matters that the shoes are gone

4   Read this sentence from the passage.

> **To Celine, self-appointed Student Police Officer and Most Qualified Detective, Mark's statement was just as good as a confession.**

What does the word *self-appointed* reveal about Celine's role?

Ⓐ   She cares a lot about the role.

Ⓑ   She gave the role to herself.

Ⓒ   She was voted into the role.

Ⓓ   She finds the role stressful.

5   In which sentence would Mark probably sound serious and determined?

Ⓐ   *"Why are you looking at me?" Mark asked Celine.*

Ⓑ   *Mark thought about that a moment, then looked down at where the shoes used to be, "You think I did this?"*

Ⓒ   *"Yeah, but I wouldn't have said anything if I really did it!"*

Ⓓ   *"I didn't take the shoes, Celine."*

6   The passage describes how Mark's sister Erin "jumped to his defense." This phrase means that she –

Ⓐ   stood up for Mark

Ⓑ   raced over to Mark

Ⓒ   asked Mark if he did it

Ⓓ   blamed Mark for the problem

7 According to the passage, why does Celine decide that Mark didn't take the shoes?

Ⓐ   His own shoes are also missing.

Ⓑ   He has no use for twenty pairs of shoes.

Ⓒ   He says that he had nothing to do with it.

Ⓓ   He was in the dance class the whole time.

8 According to the passage, the shoes of which student were most worth stealing? Select the **one** best answer.

☐   Arthur

☐   Celine

☐   Erin

☐   Mark

☐   Marvin

9 Which part of Celine's class display most likely inspires the art class to make the mobile?

Ⓐ   the title "Great Explorers"

Ⓑ   the pictures of famous explorers

Ⓒ   the maps

Ⓓ   the cut-out footprints

10   What does the photograph of Celine at the end of the passage most likely represent?

    Ⓐ   the point when she figures out where the shoes are

    Ⓑ   the point when she gives up on finding all the shoes

    Ⓒ   the point when she first notices that the shoes are missing

    Ⓓ   the point when she thinks of all the people that could have done it

11   After Celine guesses where all the shoes are, she goes to the art class. Describe **two** details about how Celine goes about this that show that she is determined.

    1: _____

    _____

    2: _____

    _____

12   The way Celine is described in the passage mainly makes her seem like –

    Ⓐ   an artist

    Ⓑ   a joker

    Ⓒ   a leader

    Ⓓ   a villain

13 At the beginning of the passage, Celine says that Mark has a motive. What is Mark's motive? Use **two** details from the passage to support your answer.

_____

_____

_____

_____

14 How do the "ideas windows" explain why the shoes have gone missing? Use **two** details from the passage to support your answer.

_____

_____

_____

_____

15 In the passage, Celine takes on the role of detective. Describe **three** ways that Celine acts like a detective. Use details from the passage in your answer.

_____

_____

_____

_____

_____

_____

_____

_____

_____

_____

_____

_____

_____

_____

_____

Practice Set 11

Legend

Antonio Canova

Instructions

This set has one passage for you to read. The passage is followed by questions.

Read each question carefully. For each multiple choice question, fill in the circle for the correct answer. For other types of questions, follow the instructions given. Some of the questions require a written answer. Write your answer on the lines provided.

Antonio Canova was an Italian artist in the late 1700s and early 1800s. He became most famous for his marble sculptures. He is often thought of as one of the greatest sculptors of his time. This Italian legend tells of Antonio as a boy. This legend is generally thought to be fiction, though the story may have been told and retold in Canova's time and presented as if it were true.

Antonio Canova
An Italian Legend

A good many years ago there lived in Italy a little boy whose name was Antonio Canova. He lived with his grandfather. His grandfather was a stonecutter, and he was very poor.

Antonio was a puny lad, and not strong enough to work. He did not care to play with the other boys of the town. But he liked to go with his grandfather to the stone-yard. While the old man was busy, cutting and trimming the great blocks of stone, the lad would play among the chips. Sometimes he would make a little statue of soft clay; sometimes he would take hammer and chisel, and try to cut a statue from a piece of rock. He showed so much skill that his grandfather was delighted.

"The boy will be a sculptor someday," he said.

Then when they went home in the evening, the grandmother would say, "What have you been doing today, my little sculptor?"

And she would take him upon her lap and sing to him, or tell him stories that filled his mind with pictures of wonderful and beautiful things. And the next day, when he went back to the stone-yard, he would try to make some of those pictures in stone or clay.

There lived in the same town a rich man who was called the Count. Sometimes the Count would have a grand dinner, and his rich friends from other towns would come to visit him. Then Antonio's grandfather would go up to the Count's house to help with the work in the kitchen; for he was a fine cook as well as a good stonecutter.

It happened one day that Antonio went with his grandfather to the Count's great house. Some people from the city were coming, and there was to be a grand feast. The boy could not cook, and he was not old enough to wait on the table; but he could wash the pans and kettles, and as he was smart and quick, he could help in many other ways.

All went well until it was time to spread the table for dinner. Then there was a crash in the dining room, and a servant rushed into the kitchen with some pieces of marble in his hands. He was pale, and trembling with fright.

"What shall I do? What shall I do?" he cried. "I have broken the statue that was to stand at the center of the table. I cannot make the table look pretty without the statue. What will the Count say?"

And now all the other servants were in trouble. Was the dinner to be a failure after all? For everything depended on having the table nicely arranged. The Count would be very angry.

"Ah, what shall we do?" they all asked.

Then little Antonio Canova left his pans and kettles, and went up to the man.

"If you had another statue, could you arrange the table?" he asked.

"Certainly," said the man; "that is, if the statue were of the right length and height."

"Will you let me try to make one?" asked Antonio. "Perhaps I can make something that will do."

The man laughed.

"Nonsense!" he cried. "Who are you that you talk of making statues on an hour's notice?"

"I am Antonio Canova," said the lad.

"Let the boy try what he can do," said the servants.

And so, since nothing else could be done, the man allowed him to try.

On the kitchen table there was a large square lump of yellow butter. Two hundred pounds the lump weighed, and it had just come in, fresh and clean, from the dairy on the mountain. With a kitchen knife in his hand, Antonio began to cut and carve this butter. In a few minutes he had molded it into the shape of a crouching lion; and all the servants crowded around to see it.

"How beautiful!" they cried. "It is a great deal prettier than the statue that was broken."

When it was finished, the man carried it to its place.

"The table will be handsomer by half than I ever hoped to make it," he said.

When the Count and his friends came in to dinner, the first thing they saw was the yellow lion.

"What a beautiful work of art!" one of the guests cried. "None but a very great artist could ever carve such a figure. And how odd that he should choose to make it of butter!" And then he asked the Count to tell them the name of the artist.

"Truly, my friends," he said, "this is as much of a surprise to me as to you." And then he called to his head servant, and asked him where he had found so wonderful a statue.

"It was carved only an hour ago by a little boy in the kitchen," said the servant.

This made the Count's friends wonder still more; and the Count bade the servant call the boy into the room.

"My lad," he said, "you have done a piece of work of which the greatest artists would be proud. What is your name, and who is your teacher?"

"My name is Antonio Canova," said the boy, "and I have had no teacher but my grandfather the stonecutter."

By this time all the guests had crowded around Antonio. There were famous artists among them, and they knew that the lad was a genius. They could not say enough in praise of his work; and when at last they sat down at the table, nothing would please them but that Antonio should have a seat with them; and the dinner was made a feast in his honor.

The very next day the Count sent for Antonio to come and live with him. The best artists in the land were employed to teach him the art in which he had shown so much skill; but now, instead of carving butter, he chiseled marble. In a few years, Antonio Canova became known as one of the greatest sculptors in the world.

1   Which sentence from the introduction best supports the idea that Antonio Canova was a talented artist?

    Ⓐ   *Antonio Canova was an Italian artist in the late 1700s and early 1800s.*

    Ⓑ   *He became most famous for his marble sculptures.*

    Ⓒ   *He is often thought of as one of the greatest sculptors of his time.*

    Ⓓ   *This Italian legend tells of Antonio as a boy.*

2   Read this sentence from the passage.

Antonio was a puny lad, and not strong enough to work.

What does the word *puny* mean?

    Ⓐ   kind and caring

    Ⓑ   small and weak

    Ⓒ   rough and rude

    Ⓓ   unique and different

3   Describe **two** ways that Antonio practiced creating artwork while in the stone-yard with his grandfather.

1: _____

_____

2: _____

_____

4   Why does the grandfather take Antonio to the Count's house?

    Ⓐ   to teach Antonio useful work skills

    Ⓑ   to introduce Antonio to the Count

    Ⓒ   to show off Antonio's skills as an artist

    Ⓓ   to have Antonio help with the work

5   Read these sentences from the passage.

> **All went well until it was time to spread the table for dinner. Then there was a crash in the dining room, and a servant rushed into the kitchen with some pieces of marble in his hands. He was pale, and trembling with fright.**
>
> **"What shall I do? What shall I do?" he cried. "I have broken the statue that was to stand at the center of the table. I cannot make the table look pretty without the statue. What will the Count say?"**

List **three** details the author includes to show how upset the servant is.

1: _____

2: _____

3: _____

6   Read these sentences from the passage.

> **"Nonsense!" he cried. "Who are you that you talk of making statues on an hour's notice?"**
>
> **"I am Antonio Canova," said the lad.**

Antonio's response mainly suggests that he is –

Ⓐ   confident

Ⓑ   confused

Ⓒ   embarrassed

Ⓓ   nervous

7   Read this sentence spoken by one of the Count's guests.

> **None but a very great artist could ever carve such a figure.**

What does this sentence mean?

Ⓐ   It must have been created by a great artist.

Ⓑ   It must have been made with great care.

Ⓒ   It must have been done by someone young.

Ⓓ   It must have been completed in a hurry.

8   The passage describes many people praising Antonio's work. Whose praise best shows the reader that Antonio really does have great talent?

    Ⓐ   the Count

    Ⓑ   the servants

    Ⓒ   famous artists

    Ⓓ   Antonio's grandparents

9   Select the **two** details from the passage that best show that Antonio's work in creating the statue is impressive.

    ☐   It is made from butter.

    ☐   It is very large.

    ☐   It was carved quickly.

    ☐   It is used as a centerpiece.

    ☐   It is the right length and height.

10   What does the legend tell overall?

    Ⓐ   how Antonio worked hard

    Ⓑ   how Antonio did not fit in

    Ⓒ   how Antonio came up with ideas

    Ⓓ   how Antonio's talent was discovered

11   Do Antonio's grandparents support him in his interest in art? Use **two** details from the passage to support your answer.

_____

_____

_____

_____

_____

12   How does the marble statue breaking create an opportunity for Antonio? Use **two** details from the passage to support your answer.

_____

_____

_____

_____

13   When Antonio offers to make a statue, the servant laughs at him. Why do you think the servant reacts like this? Explain your answer.

_____

_____

_____

_____

14   What does the last paragraph show about how the Count helps Antonio? Use **two** details from the passage to support your answer.

_____

_____

_____

_____

15 How does the dinner party change Antonio's life? Use **three** details from the passage in your answer.

_____

_____

_____

_____

_____

_____

_____

_____

_____

_____

_____

_____

_____

_____

_____

_____

Practice Set 12

Personal Narrative

My First Day at Mayfield Elementary School

Instructions

This set has one passage for you to read. The passage is followed by questions.

Read each question carefully. For each multiple choice question, fill in the circle for the correct answer. For other types of questions, follow the instructions given. Some of the questions require a written answer. Write your answer on the lines provided.

My First Day at Mayfield Elementary School
By Deena Murray

Some time ago, my family moved into a new house. We stayed in the same city, but we moved to a new suburb miles away. Because we moved, I had to change schools. My old school was just too far away to travel to every day. That was what Mom said when I begged her to let me catch a bus or a train to the school I knew so well. Every time I thought about this new unknown place, I was terrified. I had good friends at my old school. I had known most of my friends since the day we all started school together. I would now have to make new ones. I would be going to a school full of complete strangers.

My first day of school started out as scary as I had imagined. I was a bundle of nerves! I didn't know anybody – not even the teachers. When I got shown around the school, I tried to remember where everything was. But it was a lot bigger than my old school, and all the halls and classrooms looked the same. I felt too shy to ask for directions, so I just stumbled around.

I had to get used to my new class and classmates. My new class looked very different. I sat right up the back and tried to blend in. I felt like I just needed some time to watch everyone and try to feel comfortable in this new place. I also had to start learning new things and catching up on some work that I missed. I put up my hand when I was unsure about something and the teacher helped me a lot. She was very kind and gave me lots of help.

At lunchtime, I wasn't sure where to sit. Luckily, this girl named Brianna came and asked me to sit with her and her friends. They were a bubbly group of people and they made me feel welcome. They promised to look out for me. Brianna answered any questions I had and told me about all the fun things that happen at the school. I really appreciated her help. We also played some fun games at lunch, which helped me to relax. After feeling so tense all morning, it was nice to let loose and smile for a while.

After school, Dad left work early and came to pick me up. He asked me how my day was. I told him that it had been a bit frightening to start off with. But after meeting Brianna, everything got better. I still felt nervous and a little out of place, but I also felt like I would figure it all out and feel at home there soon.

Dad picked me up from school every day for my first week. It was great to see his calm face waiting by the gate. Every day, I was proud to tell him that I was feeling better all the time. I think he felt bad that he had moved our family and made me start over at a new school. I didn't want him to worry about me. So every day, I made sure to walk confidently out of school with a big smile on my face. At the end of the first week, I wasn't even faking that confidence anymore! Even though there were still a lot of new things to get used to, I felt confident that I could handle it all.

After the first week, I told Dad that I was ready to start catching the bus. I had lived close enough to my old school that Mom and I walked there and back each day. My new school was a little too far to walk, so I would now have to catch the bus instead. Dad agreed that I was ready, and told me how pleased he was. He said it was brave to accept all these changes without letting my fear stop me. I shrugged and pretended I wasn't afraid at all.

"It's just a school bus full of kids like me," I said with a laugh. "There's nothing scary about that."

Just a week ago, the idea of a bus full of strangers seemed terrifying. Now I felt a little nervous, but mostly okay. I just reminded myself that there were probably new friends to be made on that bus. It's amazing how a little bit of positive thinking can change how you see things!

Now I love my new school and have many great friends. I realize now how important it is to welcome new students. Every time a new student starts at Mayfield Elementary School, I make sure I introduce myself to her. I also show her around the school and ask her to sit with me. It feels great to be doing something nice for someone else. Of course, Brianna is always very friendly as well and she helps me get to know the new person. We are like the school's welcoming squad! It's a role I am happy to take on because I know it makes someone's difficult day a little easier.

1   Read this sentence from the passage.

> **Some time ago, my family moved into a new house.**

Which of these would best replace the phrase "Some time ago," to be more specific about when the events took place?

Ⓐ   Last August,

Ⓑ   To my surprise,

Ⓒ   In a tough year,

Ⓓ   Many moons ago,

2   Read this sentence from the first paragraph.

> **I had known most of my friends since the day we all started school together.**

What does this detail mainly help explain?

Ⓐ   why Deena has to change schools

Ⓑ   why Deena should see the change as a good thing

Ⓒ   why Deena feels nervous about making new friends

Ⓓ   why Deena is able to fit into her new school so easily

3   In paragraph 2, Deena states that she was "a bundle of nerves." This means that she felt –

Ⓐ   confused

Ⓑ   excited

Ⓒ   prepared

Ⓓ   stressed

4 Based on the details in the second paragraph, list **two** details that explain why Deena felt lost at the new school.

1: _____

_____

2: _____

_____

5 Select the **two** sentences from the third paragraph that show that Deena does not want anyone to notice her.

☐　I had to get used to my new class and classmates.

☐　My new class looked very different.

☐　I sat right up the back and tried to blend in.

☐　I felt like I just needed some time to watch everyone and try to feel comfortable in this new place.

☐　I also had to start learning new things and catching up on some work that I missed.

☐　I put up my hand when I was unsure about something and the teacher helped me a lot.

☐　She was very kind and gave me lots of help.

6   Based on the details in paragraph 4, list **two** more ways that Brianna helps Deena.

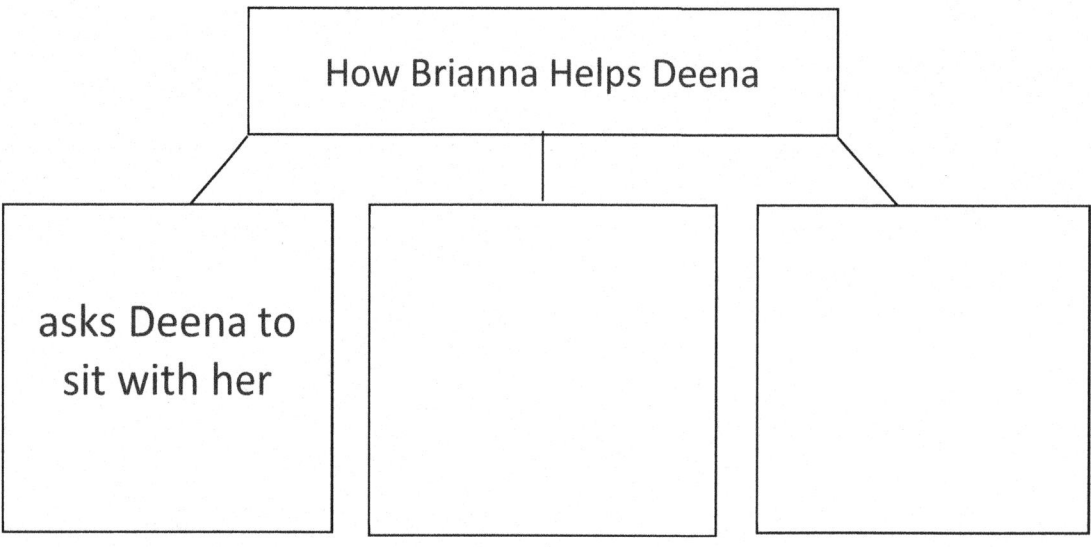

7   How does playing games at lunch help Deena?

Ⓐ   It helps her feel more relaxed.

Ⓑ   It is a way to meet new people.

Ⓒ   It reminds her that the new school is not that different.

Ⓓ   It allows her to show off her skills and feel important.

8   Which **two** phrases from paragraph 5 suggest that Deena is hopeful? Select the **two** best answers.

☐   pick me up

☐   a bit frightening

☐   still felt nervous

☐   out of place

☐   figure it all out

☐   feel at home there soon

9   Read these sentences from the passage.

Just a week ago, the idea of a bus full of strangers seemed terrifying. Now I felt a little nervous, but mostly okay.

Which statement best describes how the sentences are related?

Ⓐ   They describe a problem and its solution.

Ⓑ   They give two different people's opinions.

Ⓒ   They compare how things are now with how they were before.

Ⓓ   They describe an event and what happened because of the event.

10   Based on the passage, what makes the biggest difference to Deena's first day of school?

    Ⓐ   having her father pick her up

    Ⓑ   finding a helpful teacher

    Ⓒ   making a new friend

    Ⓓ   not getting lost

11   According to the passage, why did Deena have to change schools? Use **two** details from the passage to support your answer.

_____

_____

_____

_____

_____

12   Why does Deena leave school looking happy and confident even when she doesn't feel that way? Explain your answer.

_____

_____

_____

_____

_____

13   Deena describes Brianna and herself as the school's "welcoming squad." List **three** things Deena does to help new students.

1: _____

2: _____

3: _____

14   Deena describes how she tells her father that she is ready to start catching the bus. How does this part of the passage show that Deena's father is proud of her? Use **two** details from the passage to support your answer.

_____

_____

_____

_____

_____

15 How does Deena's experience of changing schools inspire her to help others? Use **three** details from the passage in your answer.

_____

_____

_____

_____

_____

_____

_____

_____

_____

_____

_____

_____

_____

_____

_____

_____

Practice Set 13

Play

Waste Not, Want Not

Instructions

This set has one passage for you to read. The passage is followed by questions.

Read each question carefully. For each multiple choice question, fill in the circle for the correct answer. For other types of questions, follow the instructions given. Some of the questions require a written answer. Write your answer on the lines provided.

Waste Not, Want Not

Mr. Jones: Boys, if you have nothing to do, will you unpack these parcels for me?

The two parcels were both well tied up with good whipcord. Ben took his parcel to the table, and began to examine the knot, and then to untie it.

John took the other parcel, and tried first at one corner, and then at the other, to pull off the string. But the cord had been too well secured, and he only drew the knots tighter.

John: I wish these people would not tie up their parcels so tightly, as if they were never to be undone. Why, Ben, how did you get yours undone? What is in your parcel? I wonder what is in mine! I wish I could get the string off. I will cut it.

Ben: Oh, no, do not cut it, John! Look, what a nice cord this is, and yours is the same. It is a pity to cut it.

John: Pooh! What's so important about a bit of thread?

Ben: It is whipcord.

John: Well, whipcord then! What's so important about a bit of whipcord? You can get a piece of whipcord twice as long as that for three cents; and who cares for three cents? Not I, for one. So, here it goes.

So John took out his knife, and cut it in several places.

Mr. Jones: Well, my boys, have you undone the parcels for me?

John: Yes, sir; here is the parcel.

Ben: And here is my parcel, father, and here is also the string.

Mr. Jones: You may keep the string, Ben.

Ben: Thank you, sir. What excellent whipcord it is!

Mr. Jones: And you, John, may keep your string, too, if it will be of any use to you.

John: It will be of no use to me, thank you, sir.

Mr. Jones: No, I am afraid not, if this is it.

A few weeks after this, Mr. Jones gave each of his sons a new top.

John: How is this, Ben? These tops have no strings. What shall we do for strings?

Ben: I have a string that will do very well for mine.

Ben pulled the string out of his pocket.

John: Why, if that is not the whipcord! I wish I had saved mine.

A few days afterward, there was a shooting match, with bows and arrows, among the lads. The prize was a fine bow and arrows, to be given to the best marksman.

Master Sharp: Come, come. I am within one inch of the mark. I should like to see who will go nearer.

John drew his bow, and shot. The arrow struck within a quarter of an inch of Master Sharp's.

Master Sharp: Shoot away, but you must understand the rules. We settled them before you came. You are to have three shots with your own arrows. Nobody is to borrow or lend.

John seized his second arrow, but just as we was preparing to take his shot the string broke, and the arrow fell from his hands.

Master Sharp: There! It is all over with you.

Ben: Here is my bow for him. He is welcome to use it.

Master Sharp: No, no, sir; that is not fair. Did you not hear the rules? There is to be no lending.

It was now Ben's turn to make his trial. His first arrow missed the mark; the second was exactly as near as John's first. Before shooting the last arrow, Ben carefully examined the string of his bow; and, as he pulled it to try its strength, it snapped. Master Sharp clapped his hands and danced for joy. But his dancing suddenly ceased, when Ben drew out of his pocket an excellent piece of cord, and began to tie it to the bow. Master Sharp now frowned and crossed his arms.

John: The everlasting whipcord, I declare!

Ben: Yes. I put it in my pocket, because I thought I might want it.

Ben's last arrow won the prize; and when the bow and arrows were handed to him, John congratulated him.

John: How valuable that whipcord has been to you, Ben. I'll take care how I waste anything hereafter.

1 What is Mr. Jones doing in the first line of the play?

Ⓐ giving the boys a warning

Ⓑ asking the boys a favor

Ⓒ telling the boys a story

Ⓓ teaching the boys a lesson

2 Read this sentence from the play.

> *John took the other parcel, and tried first at one corner, and then at the other, to pull off the string.*

Which word could replace the word *pull* to show that John pulled the string roughly?

Ⓐ pressed

Ⓑ slipped

Ⓒ twisted

Ⓓ yanked

3 At the beginning of the play, why is John frustrated with his parcel?

Ⓐ It is too heavy.

Ⓑ He cannot open it.

Ⓒ He wants to know what is in it.

Ⓓ He thinks Ben has something better.

4   List **two** details from the play that show that Ben is very careful with his parcel.

1: _____

_____

2: _____

_____

5   Read this line from the play.

Ben: Thank you, sir. What excellent whipcord it is!

This line mainly shows that Ben is –

Ⓐ   cautious

Ⓑ   confident

Ⓒ   grateful

Ⓓ   surprised

6   Read this sentence that describes the shooting match.

The prize was a fine bow and arrows, to be given to the best marksman.

Why is this detail important in the play?

Ⓐ   It explains why everyone is keen to win.

Ⓑ   It tells why the whipcord will be needed.

Ⓒ   It shows how Ben feels about the contest.

Ⓓ   It suggests that the contest has important rules.

7   When describing the rules of the shooting contest, Master Sharp says that "we settled them before you came." What does the phrase "settled them" mean?

    Ⓐ   They changed them.

    Ⓑ   They agreed on them.

    Ⓒ   They wrote them down.

    Ⓓ   They argued about them.

8   When John's bow breaks, Ben offers to lend him his own bow. What quality of Ben's does this mainly emphasize? Select the **one** best answer.

☐ creativity   ☐ kindness

☐ cunning   ☐ loyalty

☐ friendliness   ☐ slyness

☐ honesty   ☐ strength

9   Read this line from the play.

John: The everlasting whipcord, I declare!

How would John most likely sound when saying this line?

    Ⓐ   annoyed

    Ⓑ   jealous

    Ⓒ   impressed

    Ⓓ   shocked

10   In the last line, John describes the whipcord as having been valuable to Ben. As it is used in the line, the word *valuable* mainly describes how the whipcord has been –

Ⓐ   costly

Ⓑ   loved

Ⓒ   tough

Ⓓ   useful

11   How do John's words at the start of the play show that he doesn't care about the whipcord? Use **two** details from the play to support your answer.

_____

_____

_____

_____

12   Why does John regret not keeping his string when the father gives the boys tops? Explain your answer.

_____

_____

_____

_____

13 When Ben's string snaps, the author reveals Master Sharp's feelings by describing his actions. Complete the table by listing **two** actions that show his happiness when the string first snaps, and **two** actions that show his unhappiness when he sees that Ben can fix his bow.

Actions that Show Master Sharp's Feelings

Happiness when the String Snaps	Unhappiness when Ben Fixes the Bow
1)	1)
2)	2)

14 What does the last line of the play show about how John has changed? Use **two** details from the play to support your answer.

_____

_____

_____

_____

_____

15 How do Ben's and John's actions teach the reader about appreciating things? Use **three** details from the play in your answer.

_____

_____

_____

_____

_____

_____

_____

_____

_____

_____

_____

_____

_____

_____

_____

_____

_____

Practice Set 14

Poetry

Set of Two Poems

Instructions

This set has two passages for you to read. Each passage is followed by questions.

Read each question carefully. For each multiple choice question, fill in the circle for the correct answer. For other types of questions, follow the instructions given. Some of the questions require a written answer. Write your answer on the lines provided.

The Grasshopper and the Ant

The grasshopper, singing
All summer long,
Now found winter stinging,
And ceased in his song.
Not a morsel or crumb in his cupboard –
So he shivered, and ceased in his song.

Miss Ant was his neighbor;
To her he went:
"Oh, you're rich from labor,
And I've not a cent.
Lend me food, and I vow I'll return it,
Though at present I have not a cent."

The ant's not a lender,
I must confess.
Her heart's far from tender
To one in distress.
So she said: "Pray, how passed you the summer,
That in winter you come to distress?"

"I sang through the summer,"
the grasshopper said.
"But now I am glummer
Because I've no bread."
"So you *sang!*" sneered the Ant. "That relieves me.
Now it's winter – go *dance* for your bread!"

1   Read this line from the poem.

Now found winter stinging,

This line means that the grasshopper found winter –

Ⓐ   confusing

Ⓑ   difficult

Ⓒ   exciting

Ⓓ   tiring

2   Which line from the first stanza tells the grasshopper's main problem? Select the **one** best answer.

☐   The grasshopper, singing

☐   All summer long,

☐   Now found winter stinging,

☐   And ceased in his song.

☐   Not a morsel or crumb in his cupboard –

☐   So he shivered, and ceased in his song.

3   What is the grasshopper doing in the second stanza of the poem?

    Ⓐ   asking the ant for help

    Ⓑ   making fun of the ant

    Ⓒ   trying to trick the ant

    Ⓓ   entertaining the ant

4   Read these lines from the poem.

> **Her heart's far from tender**
> **To one in distress.**

What do these lines show about the ant?

    Ⓐ   She is not caring.

    Ⓑ   She is not friendly.

    Ⓒ   She is not patient.

    Ⓓ   She is not talkative.

5   Read this statement from the ant from the last stanza.

> **"So you *sang*!" sneered the Ant.**

The way the ant speaks suggests that she is –

    Ⓐ   annoyed

    Ⓑ   puzzled

    Ⓒ   understanding

    Ⓓ   unimpressed

6   Which detail best explains how you can tell that "The Grasshopper and the Ant" is a narrative poem?

    Ⓐ   It uses rhyme.

    Ⓑ   It has a message.

    Ⓒ   It tells a story.

    Ⓓ   It is divided into stanzas.

7   The main message of the poem is about –

    Ⓐ   accepting change

    Ⓑ   having a talent

    Ⓒ   showing kindness

    Ⓓ   preparing for the future

8   What does the illustration show about how the grasshopper and the ant spent their summer? Use **two** details from the illustration to support your answer.

_____

_____

_____

_____

_____

9   How do the grasshopper's actions lead to his problem? Use **two** details from the poem to support your answer.

_____

_____

_____

_____

_____

10   Why do you think the ant chooses not to help the grasshopper? Explain your answer.

_____

_____

_____

_____

When Father Carves the Duck
By E.V. Wright

We all look on with anxious eyes
When Father carves the duck,
And Mother almost always sighs
When Father carves the duck;
Then all of us prepare to rise
And hold our bibs before our eyes,
And be prepared for some surprise
When Father carves the duck.

He braces up and grabs the fork,
Whene'er he carves the duck,
And won't allow a soul to talk
Until he carves the duck.
The fork is jabbed into the sides,
Across the breast the knife he slides,
While every careful person hides
From flying chips of duck.

The platter's always sure to slip
When Father carves the duck,
And how it makes the dishes skip—
Potatoes fly amuck.
The squash and cabbage leap in space,
We get some gravy in our face,
And Father mutters in disgrace
Whene'er he carves a duck.

We then have learned to walk around
The dining room and pluck
From off the window-sills and walls
Our share of Father's duck.
While Father growls and blows and jaws,
And swears the knife was full of flaws,
And Mother laughs at him because
He couldn't carve a duck.

1 Read this line from the poem.

      We all look on with anxious eyes

What does the line mean?

   Ⓐ   We all sit quietly.

   Ⓑ   We all watch nervously.

   Ⓒ   We all wait patiently.

   Ⓓ   We all stare hungrily.

2 The second stanza describes how the fork is "jabbed into the sides." The word *jabbed* suggests that the fork is poked into the duck –

   Ⓐ   roughly

   Ⓑ   carefully

   Ⓒ   quietly

   Ⓓ   firmly

3 Complete the diagram below by listing all the food that makes a mess other than the duck.

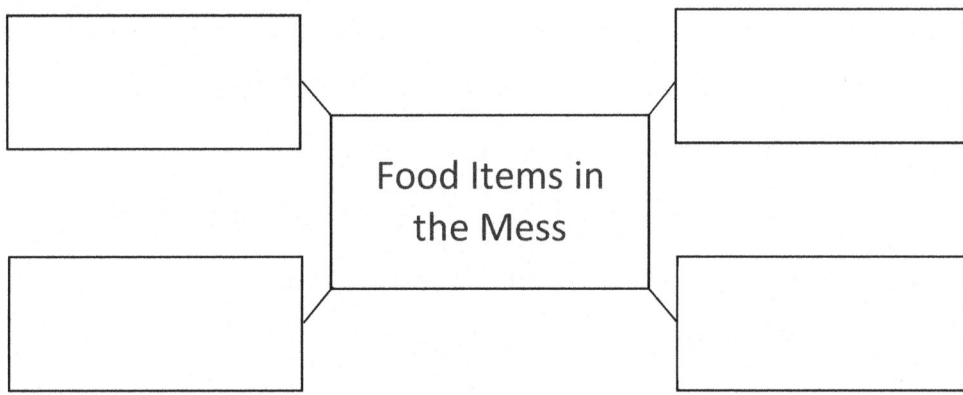

4 Read this line from the last stanza.

And swears the knife was full of flaws,

What does this line show about the father?

Ⓐ   He blames the knife.

Ⓑ   He throws the knife away.

Ⓒ   He sharpens the knife.

Ⓓ   He uses the same knife each time.

5 Which pair of lines from the second stanza shows that the family members expect carving the duck to go wrong?

Ⓐ   *He braces up and grabs the fork, / Whene'er he carves the duck,*

Ⓑ   *And won't allow a soul to talk / Until he carves the duck.*

Ⓒ   *The fork is jabbed into the sides, / Across the breast the knife he slides,*

Ⓓ   *While every careful person hides / From flying chips of duck.*

6 Which statement best describes how all the stanzas of the poem are related?

Ⓐ   Each stanza gives a different person's view of the event.

Ⓑ   Each stanza gives a new opinion on the event.

Ⓒ   Each stanza tells part of the event from beginning to end.

Ⓓ   Each stanza describes a different cause of the event.

7   The poem is most likely meant to –

    Ⓐ   make the reader laugh

    Ⓑ   teach the reader a lesson

    Ⓒ   encourage the reader to take action

    Ⓓ   make the reader care about a topic

8   Describe **two** details from the poem that support your answer to Question 7.

1: _____

_____

2: _____

_____

9   Complete the table by listing the word or phrase used to describe how each item moves.

Item	Words Used to Describe Its Movement
chips of duck	
platter	
dishes	
potatoes	
squash and cabbage	

10   Does the poem suggest that the family members are annoyed or amused by the events? Explain your answer.

_____

_____

_____

_____

_____

Practice Set 15

Fairy Tale

Cinderella

Instructions

This set has one passage for you to read. The passage is followed by questions.

Read each question carefully. For each multiple choice question, fill in the circle for the correct answer. For other types of questions, follow the instructions given. Some of the questions require a written answer. Write your answer on the lines provided.

Cinderella

Once upon a time there lived a maiden named Cinderella. Her mother had died long ago, and she had to work very, very hard in the kitchen. She had two older sisters, but they were cross to little Cinderella. They made her stay among the pots and the kettles and do all the hard work about the house. Sometimes, to keep warm, she crept in among the cinders. That is why she was called Cinderella.

One day the sisters came dancing into the house. They clapped their hands and twirled each other around.

"We have been invited to the king's ball," they sang.

At length the day of the great ball came, and the two sisters rode away in their fine silk dresses. Poor Cinderella, who had to stay behind, looked at her old ragged clothes, and burst into tears.

"Alas," she cried. "Why should I always have to stay in the kitchen while my sisters dress in silks and satins?"

Hardly had she spoken when there stood before her a dear little old lady with a golden wand in her hand. She had the kindest eyes that Cinderella had ever seen.

"My child," she cried, "I am your fairy godmother, and you shall go to the ball, too. First go into the garden, Cinderella, and bring to me the largest pumpkin you can find."

When Cinderella had done this, the fairy waved her golden wand over the yellow pumpkin. In a flash, it was not a pumpkin at all, but a beautiful yellow coach.

"Now bring me four white mice, two large ones and two small ones."

In a moment Cinderella brought a trap full of mice into the room. The fairy waved her golden wand, and the two largest mice were turned into two snow-white horses. Two small mice became two men, one a coachman, the other a footman.

"But how am I to go in these clothes?" said Cinderella.

"Ah, let me see," said the fairy, and she slowly waved her wand over the maiden's head.

Oh, what a change! The rags tumbled to the floor. And, what do you think! In their place was a beautiful pink silk dress. The ugly shoes fell off. And, lo! A tiny pair of glass slippers were on Cinderella's little feet.

"Now listen to what I say," said the fairy godmother. "You must not stay after the clock strikes twelve. At that time your coach will again be a pumpkin, the men will be mice, and you will have on your old ragged dress."

Cinderella said she would not forget. Then she jumped into the coach, and away she drove to the king's ball.

The king's son was charmed with Cinderella. She was so very beautiful that he would dance with her and with no one else. Cinderella had such a good time that she forgot about the clock. It began to strike twelve—one, two, three.

Cinderella ran from the room. Down the steps of the palace she flew. She ran so fast that she lost one of her little glass slippers. The clock finished striking. Lo! The coach turned into a pumpkin. The horses and men turned into mice. Poor Cinderella had to walk home in her ragged clothes.

The next morning the prince found Cinderella's little glass slipper on the stairs.

"There is only one maiden in all the world who can wear so tiny a slipper," said the prince. "I will marry her and no other."

The prince hunted far and wide for a maiden who could put it on. Hundreds of people tried, but none could do it. At last he came to the house where Cinderella lived. The two older sisters tried to put the slipper on their large feet. Then Cinderella came into the room.

"Let me try it," she said.

"You!" cried the older sisters. "You could never put it on."

"Let her try it," said the prince.

At once the little glass slipper was fitted to the tiny foot. Then Cinderella stood up and her ragged clothes turned into a beautiful silk dress, and there were two little slippers on her two little feet. Then the prince knew that Cinderella was the one he had danced with at the ball, and taking her hand, he led her out to his coach.

Soon they were married and lived happily ever after.

1   What is the main purpose of the first paragraph?

Ⓐ   to explain the main problem

Ⓑ   to introduce the main character

Ⓒ   to describe the setting

Ⓓ   to tell the message of the story

2   The illustration of Cinderella at the beginning of the passage mainly shows –

Ⓐ   how Cinderella longs to find a prince

Ⓑ   how miserable Cinderella feels

Ⓒ   how mean Cinderella's sisters are

Ⓓ   how Cinderella was named

3   How do the two older sisters feel when they are invited to the king's ball?

Ⓐ   amused

Ⓑ   excited

Ⓒ   nervous

Ⓓ   proud

4   List **two** details from the passage that support your answer to Question 3.

1: _____

_____

2: _____

_____

5   Read this sentence from the passage.

> **Poor Cinderella, who had to stay behind, looked at her old ragged clothes, and burst into tears.**

The word *ragged* shows that the clothes are –

Ⓐ   old and torn

Ⓑ   light and breezy

Ⓒ   heavy and uncomfortable

Ⓓ   dirty and smelly

6   Read this question asked by Cinderella.

> **"Why should I always have to stay in the kitchen while my sisters dress in silks and satins?"**

Based on asking this question, how does Cinderella feel?

Ⓐ   embarrassed

Ⓑ   guilty

Ⓒ   jealous

Ⓓ   confused

7 Which detail from the passage suggests that the fairy godmother is going to use magic?

Ⓐ She is a dear little old lady.

Ⓑ She is carrying a golden wand.

Ⓒ She has very kind eyes.

Ⓓ She says that Cinderella will go to the ball.

8 Complete the diagram below by listing what each item is turned into.

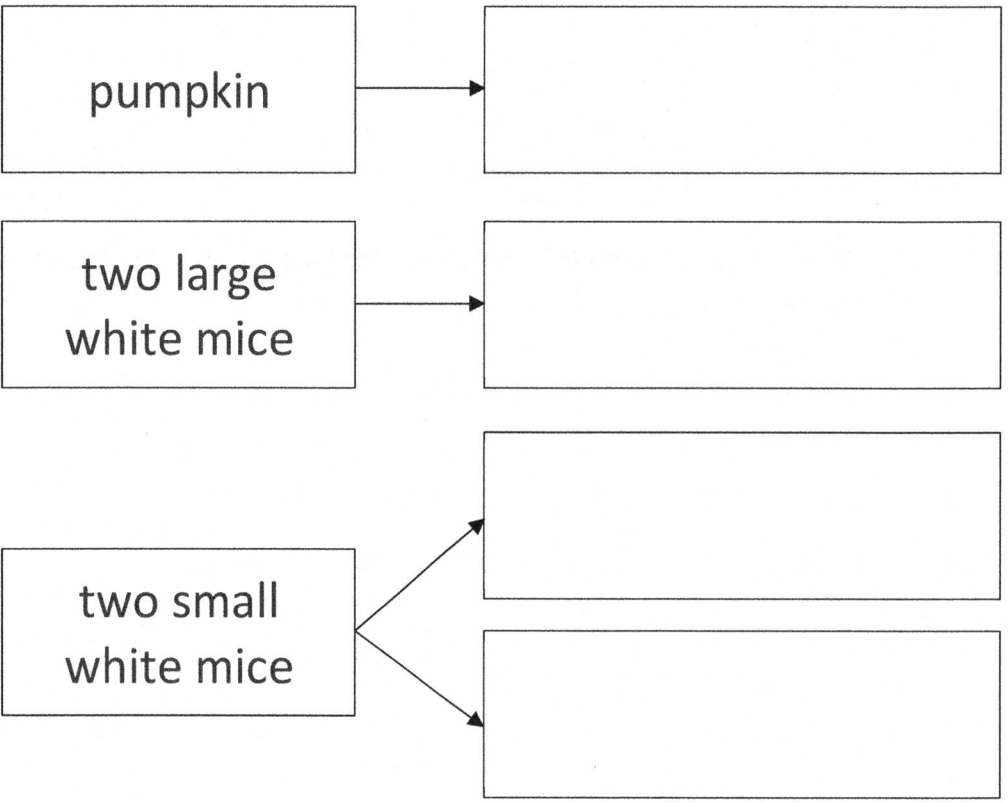

9 Read these sentences from the passage.

> **"You must not stay after the clock strikes twelve. At that time your coach will again be a pumpkin, the men will be mice, and you will have on your old ragged dress."**

Which word best describes these sentences?

Ⓐ opinion

Ⓑ question

Ⓒ summary

Ⓓ warning

10 Which sentence best describes what the illustration on the second page shows?

Ⓐ *The king's son was charmed with Cinderella.*

Ⓑ *She was so very beautiful that he would dance with her and with no one else.*

Ⓒ *Cinderella had such a good time that she forgot about the clock.*

Ⓓ *It began to strike twelve—one, two, three.*

11 How does the fairy godmother use magic to help Cinderella? Use **two** details from the passage in your answer.

_____

_____

_____

_____

_____

12   The passage describes how the prince finds Cinderella's slipper. Why is this important to the events of the story? Use **two** details from the passage in your answer.

_____

_____

_____

_____

_____

13   List **two** details that show how determined the prince is to find Cinderella.

1: _____

_____

2: _____

_____

14   How do the two older sisters most likely feel when the slipper fits Cinderella? Explain your answer.

_____

_____

_____

_____

_____

15 One common feature of fairy tales is that they often have happy endings. Describe how the story of Cinderella is an example of this. Use details from the passage to support your response.

_____

_____

_____

_____

_____

_____

_____

_____

_____

_____

_____

_____

_____

_____

_____

_____

Practice Set 16

Historical Fiction

Betty's Reward

Instructions

This set has one passage for you to read. The passage is followed by questions.

Read each question carefully. For each multiple choice question, fill in the circle for the correct answer. For other types of questions, follow the instructions given. Some of the questions require a written answer. Write your answer on the lines provided.

Betty's Reward

Betty lived a long, long time ago on a farm in North Carolina. She knew how to clean up the house, to wash the dishes, to sew, and to cook. She knew how to knit, and to spin and weave, too.

One day Betty's father said, "Let us go to town tomorrow. President Washington is passing through the South, and a man told me today that he will be in Salisbury tomorrow."

"Yes," said Betty's brother Robert, "and our company has been asked to march in the parade. One of the boys is going to make a speech of welcome."

"I should like to go," said their mother, "but I can't leave home."

"Oh, yes, you can, mother," said Betty. "I have stayed here by myself many times, and I can stay tomorrow. You go with father, and I will take care of things."

The next morning everyone on the place was up before the sun. Robert was so impatient to start to town that he could scarcely eat any breakfast. Mother was so excited that she forgot to put coffee in the coffee pot. Father must have looked at his pocket watch at least a dozen times.

At last everyone had left, and Betty was alone. "I wish I could see the President," she said, "and I do wish I could see his great coach. Father says that it is finer than the Governor's. Four men ride in front of it, and four behind it. The servants are dressed in white and gold. How I wish I could see it all!"

While Betty was talking to herself, she was not idle. She washed the dishes and she cleaned the house. Then, as it was not time to get dinner, she sat down on the shady porch.

"I wonder whether General Washington looks like his picture," she said. "Oh, if I could only see him!"

But what sound was that? Betty stood up, and shading her eyes with her hands, looked down the road. Four horsemen came along at a gallop. Then there followed a great white coach, trimmed with gold and drawn by four white horses. There were four horsemen behind the coach, and last of all came several servants.

All stopped at the gate. A tall handsome man stepped from the coach and came up the walk. Betty felt as if she could neither move nor speak. She remembered, however, all that her mother had taught her, and she made a low curtsy as the gentleman reached the steps.

"Good morning, my little maid," he said. "I know it is late, but would you give an old man some breakfast?"

Betty's cheeks grew as pink as the rose by the porch. She made another curtsy and said, "Indeed, I will. I am the only one at home, for father, mother, and Robert have gone to Salisbury to see the great Washington. But I am sure I can give you some breakfast. Father says that I am a good cook."

"I know you are, and that you are as brisk as you are pretty. Just give me a breakfast, and I promise you that you shall see Washington before your father, mother, or brother Robert does."

"I will do the best I can, sir," Betty said.

The other men came in, and all sat on the porch and talked while Betty worked. Getting her mother's whitest cloth and the silver that came from England, she quickly set the table. She brought out a loaf of new bread and a jar of fresh honey. Then she ran to the spring house and got yellow butter and rich milk. She had some fresh eggs that had been laid by her own hens. These she dropped into boiling water. Last of all she cut thin slices of delicious ham.

When everything was ready, Betty went to the porch and invited the strangers in. Her cheeks were now the color of the red rose by the gate.

The visitors ate heartily of all the good things Betty had prepared. As the tall, handsome gentleman rose to go, he leaned over and kissed her on the cheek. "My pretty little cook," he said, "you may tell your brother Robert that you saw Washington before he did, and that he kissed you, too."

You may believe that Betty did tell it. She told it to everyone she knew. She told it to her children, and they told it to their children, and I am telling it to you today.

1   In paragraph 1, all the things that Betty knows how to do are listed. Circle the **one** skill listed below that is most important to the main events of the passage.

clean up the house   wash the dishes

sew   cook

knit   spin and weave

2   Based on your answer to Question 1, explain why that skill is most important.

_____

_____

_____

_____

_____

3   List **two** details from paragraph 3 that suggest that the town is excited to have Washington visit.

1: _____

_____

2: _____

_____

4   Read this dialogue from the passage.

> **"Oh, yes, you can, mother," said Betty. "I have stayed here by myself many times, and I can stay tomorrow. You go with father, and I will take care of things."**

This dialogue mainly shows that Betty is –

Ⓐ   determined

Ⓑ   patient

Ⓒ   sneaky

Ⓓ   thoughtful

5   Complete the table below by listing the detail the author includes to show how excited each family member is when they are preparing to leave to see Washington.

What Each Person Does Because They are Excited

Family Member	Detail
Robert	
Mother	
Father	

6   Read these sentences from paragraph 7.

> **"I wish I could see the President," she said, "and I do wish I could see his great coach. Father says that it is finer than the Governor's. Four men ride in front of it, and four behind it. The servants are dressed in white and gold. How I wish I could see it all!"**

What do Betty's words suggest?

Ⓐ   She is sad to be missing out.

Ⓑ   She understands that someone has to stay home.

Ⓒ   She plans to sneak into town by herself.

Ⓓ   She hopes Washington will pass by in his coach.

7   Which sentence from paragraph 7 compares and contrasts?

Ⓐ   *At last everyone had left, and Betty was alone.*

Ⓑ   *Father says that it is finer than the Governor's.*

Ⓒ   *Four men ride in front of it, and four behind it.*

Ⓓ   *The servants are dressed in white and gold.*

8   The passage describes how "Betty's cheeks grew as pink as the rose by the porch." What is this an example of?

Ⓐ   a simile

Ⓑ   a metaphor

Ⓒ   personification

Ⓓ   exaggeration

9   List **two** details that show that Betty is polite to the visitors.

1: _____

_____

2: _____

_____

10   Complete the web below by listing **six** items that Betty serves to Washington and his men.

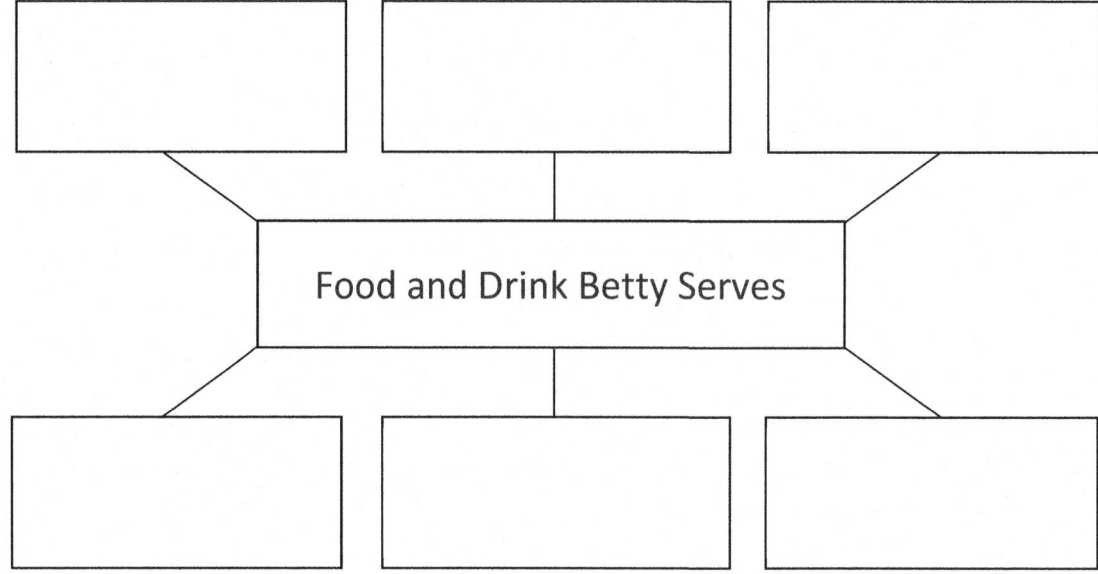

Food and Drink Betty Serves

11   Read this sentence from the passage.

> **The visitors ate heartily of all the good things Betty had prepared.**

What does the word *heartily* show?

- Ⓐ   They ate quickly.
- Ⓑ   They thanked Betty.
- Ⓒ   They enjoyed the food.
- Ⓓ   They chatted as they ate.

12   The way Betty is described in the passage suggests that children at the time were expected to –

- Ⓐ   be positive and cheerful
- Ⓑ   study and do well at school
- Ⓒ   help out around the house
- Ⓓ   spend time playing outdoors

13   Read these sentences from paragraph 10.

> **But what sound was that? Betty stood up, and shading her eyes with her hands, looked down the road. Four horsemen came along at a gallop. Then there followed a great white coach, trimmed with gold and drawn by four white horses. There were four horsemen behind the coach, and last of all came several servants.**

How do the details in this paragraph reveal to the reader that the person arriving is Washington? Explain your answer.

_____

_____

_____

_____

14   What does the last paragraph suggest about how Betty felt about the events? Explain your answer.

_____

_____

_____

_____

15 Describe **two** good deeds that Betty does. How is she rewarded for them? Use **three** details from the passage in your answer.

_____

_____

_____

_____

_____

_____

_____

_____

_____

_____

_____

_____

_____

_____

_____

_____

Answer Key

Practice Set 1
Learning Guitar

Question	Answer
1	B
2	A
3	C
4	The student should list how James's fingers became stronger and how the muscles in his hands became stronger.
5	B
6	The student should complete the diagram with the skills in the order below. chords → strumming → scales
7	A
8	B
9	A
10	determined focused
11	The student should give a reasonable description of the purpose of the simile. The answer may refer to how it helps readers imagine the sound or shows how terrible it sounded.
12	The student should relate learning the guitar to climbing a mountain. The answer may refer to how it felt slow and difficult and how it felt like you were not getting anywhere.
13	The student should describe how the author shows that playing the guitar has been an enjoyable skill to have. The answer may describe how the author plays for family and friends, how family and friends sing along, or how he plays while camping.
14	However, seeing my skills improve makes the hard work worth every moment.
15	The student should give a reasonable description of how James shows that learning the guitar was difficult and include specific examples of three difficulties. The difficulties could include how his fingers hurt at first, how learning chords was hard, how it was hard to learn strumming, or how there were many scales to learn. The answer could also refer to how he had to practice every day or how the process of learning felt slow and difficult.

Practice Set 2
Donal and Conal

Question	Answer
1	D
2	D
3	A
4	D
5	B
6	C
7	The student may list how Conal does not dance for long, speaks to the elves roughly, says it is enough, or asks if they expect him to dance all night.
8	A
9	C
10	The student may tell how Donal is curious about the dancing, amazed by the dancing, or amused by the dancing. The answer may refer to how he creeps nearer and nearer, how he laughs out loud, or how he says it is the worst dancing he has ever seen.
11	The student should complete the web with any three of the following details. The elves clap their hands. The elves make him dance again and again. The elves offer him silver. The elves offer him gold. The elves offer him diamonds.
12	The student should describe how the elves are angry with Donal before he dances and want to harm him, but are then amazed by Donal and want to give him gifts.
13	"wee bit frightened"
14	The student should explain that the queen punishes Conal by making sure he goes home without any rewards. The answer may refer to how she says "you shall have nothing" or how the gold and silver are turned to stones.
15	The student should give a reasonable explanation as to why the story has a happy ending for Donal but not Conal and use relevant supporting details. The answer may refer to how Donal is cheerful, positive, and has a good heart, while Conal is greedy, selfish, and rude. The answer may also infer that Donal dances with joy, while Conal only dances to try to make the elves give him rewards.

Practice Set 3
The Vain Jackdaw

Question	Answer
1	C
2	A
3	B
4	A
5	C
6	The student should complete the web with the details below. stay with them, walk with them, talk with them
7	B
8	THIRD PEACOCK: Let's take them from him! FIRST PEACOCK: Come, let's pull them out!
9	A
10	The student may list how the peacocks laugh at the jackdaw, call him a silly jackdaw, or laugh and say that they dropped the feathers he is wearing.
11	The student should give a reasonable explanation about why the vain jackdaw calls the peacocks "brothers." The answer may describe how he respects them, how he thinks he is one of them, how he expects the peacocks to accept him, or how he thinks that he is part of the peacock's family.
12	The student should describe how the illustration shows the vain jackdaw when he first meets the peacocks. The answer may refer to how he seems to be strutting about happily, how a peacock is watching him, or how he is still wearing the peacock feathers and has not had them plucked out yet.
13	The student should explain why the vain jackdaw wants to join the other jackdaws at the end of the play. The answer may refer to how he has been rejected and chased away by the peacocks, how he now wants to be among his own, or how he has now accepted that he is a jackdaw.
14	The student should explain that the jackdaws are repeating what the jackdaw said to them at the start of the play when he said that he did not want to walk with jackdaws, talk with jackdaws, and said that he was too fine for jackdaws.
15	The student should give a reasonable explanation of the lesson the vain jackdaw learns and support the answer with relevant details. The student may describe the vain jackdaw as learning to be humble, learning to accept himself, or learning not to focus too much on appearance.

Practice Set 4
Making History – Henry Ford

Question	Answer
1	The student should complete the web with the details below. long days in the sun, hard work, smelly farm animals
2	B
3	A
4	D
5	A
6	A
7	The student may list how orders flooded in, how they were not able to produce Model Ts fast enough, how half the cars in America were Model Ts, or how 15 million Model Ts were sold.
8	B
9	D
10	C
11	The student should describe how watches and engines both had many small parts working together to make something useful.
12	The student should list how Henry Ford increased the size of the production plant and began using a moving assembly line.
13	The student should describe how automobiles are replacing the horse and cart. The answer may refer to how gasoline will provide the power instead of horses and how the car will act as a carriage.
14	The student should complete the table with the following details. stunning white wheels, sparkling headlights, glossy paintwork
15	The student should describe how Henry Ford always wanted to make things better and use relevant supporting details. The answer may refer to how he kept improving his first automobile, how he made many changes before the Model T was ready, how he improved how the cars were manufactured, or how he designed the Model A to be even better than the Model T.

Practice Set 5
The Wolf and the Kid

Question	Answer
1	C
2	The student may list how the sun was sinking, how long shadows crept over the ground, how there was a chilly wind, how the wind came creeping, or how there were spooky noises in the grass.
3	C
4	The kid knew there was little hope for him. I know you are going to eat me.
5	D
6	A
7	The student should describe how the author helps the reader imagine the kid dancing. The answer should refer to the use of the words *leaped*, *frisked*, or *merrily*. The answer may refer to how you can imagine the kid leaping about or how you can imagine that the kid looks and feels happy and joyful.
8	The student should describe how the shepherd dogs hear the wolf singing and run back to chase the wolf away and save the kid. The answer may refer to the dogs knowing that it is the song the wolf sings before a feast or may infer that the dogs realize they have a left a kid behind or that the kid is in danger.
9	The student should explain that the wolf feels upset, annoyed, or disappointed in himself. The answer should show an understanding that the wolf wishes he had eaten the kid when he could instead of singing or playing music for him. The answer may refer to how the wolf "called himself a fool."
10	Paragraph 1

Practice Set 5
The Miller, His Son, and the Donkey

Question	Answer
1	C
2	B
3	The student may list how "a loud shout went up," how the situation is described as a crime, or how one of the people refers to loading up a poor beast.
4	D
5	The student should explain that the traveler is saying that you would expect the donkey to be the stupidest of the three, but the people are stupider than the donkey.
6	A
7	The student should explain that the company of people say that the miller and his son would be better able to carry the donkey than the donkey carry them. The answer should describe how the miller and his son listen to the people and carry the donkey into the market.
8	The student should complete the diagram with the missing steps below. The son rides the donkey. The miller rides the donkey. The miller and his son ride the donkey.
9	The student should give a reasonable description of the message of the story. The answer should refer to how the miller tried to please everybody, and how this resulted in him pleasing nobody. The message may be summarized as being about not listening to everyone's opinion, about not trying to make everyone else happy, about thinking for yourself, or about doing what you think is best instead of what other people think.
10	The student should give a reasonable example of how he or she could use the message in his or her own life. Any answer can be accepted as long as it relates the message to a real-life example.

Practice Set 6
First Day on Mars

Question	Answer
1	"all been told a million times"
2	A
3	The student may list how Andy is "gripping" the bench, how he is holding on with both hands, or how he is holding on as if he is expecting Deni to pull him away.
4	C
5	C
6	B
7	A
8	C
9	The student should complete the web with the three examples of things going wrong below. his spacesuit getting a leak, his visor cracking, a dust storm coming
10	B
11	C
12	The student should describe how the story is set on Mars and takes place in an airlock between the dome on Mars and the outside of Mars.
13	The student should give a reasonable description of how the details about kicking a football and jumping change Andy's feelings. The answer should refer to how Andy is interested in these details and starts to get excited about going outside.
14	The student should describe how putting on a spacesuit on Mars is similar to crossing the street on Earth. The answer should show an understanding that both activities can be dangerous, but are safe as long as they are done correctly. The student may explain that Deni says this to help Andy understand that he does not need to be afraid, but just needs to follow simple rules to remain safe.
15	The student should describe how Andy feels at the start of the passage and how his feelings change by the end of the passage. The answer should include relevant supporting details. The student should explain that Andy feels nervous and scared at the beginning of the passage and does not want to leave the airlock, but then feels braver and excited about leaving the airlock by the end of the passage.

Practice Set 7
A Busy Day

Question	Answer
1	A
2	C
3	B
4	D
5	B
6	The student should describe how the stanza makes the wind seem like a person rather than a thing. The answer may describe how the stanza describes the wind leaving home in the morning and tells how nobody seems to care about him.
7	The student should give a reasonable description of the image created by the lines. The answer may describe how the clouds are grouped together and how they move together like sheep being herded.
8	The student may list how the hat is "snatched" off, how it rolls on and on, how it leads to a merry chase, or how John is described as laughing and scampering.
9	B
10	B

Practice Set 7
Golden Keys

Question	Answer
1	B
2	B
3	B
4	Beg your pardon. → You bump into someone by accident. Forgive me. → You repeat some gossip you heard about someone. If you please. → You want your brother to pass you the salt at dinner. Thank you. → Your friend lends you a pen in class.
5	D
6	A
7	C
8	The student should explain that the keys represent polite phrases you say at different times or things you say to have good manners. The answer may refer to specific examples of the phrases such as "thank you," "excuse me," or "forgive me."
9	The student should describe how the girl has knocked the ice cream out of man's hand or caused the man to drop the ice cream. The student should describe how the girl is reacting by saying that she is sorry.
10	The student should describe how all the keys are similar because they are all ways of being kind.

Practice Set 8
The Poplar Tree

Question	Answer
1	A
2	The student should list the three mythical characters below. Iris, Zeus, Mercury
3	D
4	D
5	C
6	B
7	an honest mistake
8	C
9	The student should explain that the trees are not lying because they do not realize that the pot of gold is there. The answer should refer to how the thief hid the pot of gold while the trees were asleep.
10	The answer may refer to how the trees are described as if they are human, how trees do not really talk, how the passage refers to a pot of gold at the end of the rainbow, or how the passage includes mythical characters.

Practice Set 8
Why the Parrot Repeats

Question	Answer
1	A
2	D
3	B
4	The student should list how the thief pours water over the jar and how the thief hits the jar with a piece of wood.
5	The student should list how the parrot thinks it rained or that there was a storm and thinks there was thunder.
6	C
7	D
8	The student should describe how the mockingbird tells the parrot just to repeat people's words instead of telling the truth.
9	The student should explain that the thief's plan does work. The answer should refer to how the thief makes the villagers think that the parrot is lying and cannot be trusted to tell the truth, and so no longer believe that the thief stole the ox.
10	The student may list how the parrot is no longer allowed to live in people's homes, is no longer thought of as honest, or now just repeats what people say instead of telling the truth.

Practice Set 9
Josie's Journey

Question	Answer
1	B
2	D
3	C
4	A
5	The student may list how it is kept in a secret compartment, how it was given to her by a blind peddler, or how she was told she would one day need it to keep her safe.
6	inch by inch eased her way down
7	B
8	The student may list how Josie hardly dared to breathe, how she was afraid of sneezing, how she slowed her breathing, or how she counted to fifteen.
9	D
10	A
11	B
12	The student should describe how the paragraph emphasizes how strange it is that someone would be at the window. The answer should refer to how the castle is forty feet high and how Josie's room is at the top.
13	The student should give a reasonable explanation as to why Josie reacts in horror to the rope. The answer should describe how she realizes she is going to have to climb down the rope or how the thought of having to climb down the rope scares her.
14	The student should explain that Monty tells Josie to dive into the bushes to hide from the henchmen. The answer may refer to how he is acting as lookout, how Josie hides in the bushes as the men pass, or how Monty says that it was her uncle's henchmen.
15	The student should give a reasonable explanation of how you can tell that Monty and Nanny are helping Josie escape. The answer should use relevant supporting details. The answer may refer to how Monty climbs to Josie's window, how Josie escapes out her window, how Josie leaves late at night, how Nanny has clothes ready for Josie, how they hide from the henchmen, or how they take a horse from the stables and ride off.

Practice Set 10
Missing Shoes

Question	Answer
1	A
2	D
3	A
4	B
5	D
6	A
7	D
8	Erin
9	D
10	A
11	The student may list how Celine goes without asking Ms. Teleson, how she marches to the art class, or how she pushes open the door without knocking.
12	C
13	The student should explain that Mark's motive is to get out of doing the dance lessons or to get the dance classes cancelled. The answer should refer to how Mark says that he doesn't like dance and how this makes Celine think that he must have taken the shoes.
14	The student should relate the "ideas windows" to the missing shoes. The answer should describe how the students in the art class were inspired by the footprints in the window of Celine's class and took the shoes to make a mobile.
15	The student should describe three ways that Celine acts like a detective and use relevant supporting details. The answer may refer to how she tries to solve a mystery, thinks of suspects, questions people that she thinks might have done it, looks for clues, or tries to think of who might have done it and why.

Practice Set 11
Antonio Canova

Question	Answer
1	C
2	B
3	The student should list how Antonio made little statues of soft clay and how Antonio would use a hammer and chisel to try to cut a statue from a rock.
4	D
5	The student may list how the servant rushed into the kitchen, was pale, was trembling, repeats "what shall I do?", or asks what the Count will say.
6	A
7	A
8	D
9	It is made from butter. It was carved quickly.
10	D
11	The student should explain that Antonio's grandparents do support him. The answer may refer to how the grandfather says that Antonio will be a sculptor some day and how the grandmother calls Antonio "my little sculptor."
12	The student should explain that when the statue breaks a new one is needed for the table and this gives Antonio an opportunity to use his art skills or to show everyone his skills.
13	The student should give a reasonable explanation as to why the servant laughs at Antonio. The answer may infer that the servant thinks Antonio is too young or thinks that nobody could make a statue in such a short time.
14	The student should describe how the last paragraph shows that the Count has Antonio live with him and allows Antonio to be trained as an artist and sculptor.
15	The student should give a reasonable explanation of how the dinner party changes Antonio's life and use relevant supporting details. The answer should refer to how Antonio's talent is discovered, how he begins to get proper training, and how he later becomes one of the greatest sculptors in the world.

Practice Set 12
My First Day at Mayfield Elementary School

Question	Answer
1	A
2	C
3	D
4	The student may list how Deena didn't know anybody, how the school was bigger than her last one, how everything looked the same, or how she was too shy to ask for directions.
5	I sat right up the back and tried to blend in. I felt like I just needed some time to watch everyone and try to feel comfortable in this new place.
6	The student should complete the web with any two of the details below. promises to look out for Deena, answers Deena's questions, tells Deena about fun things that happen
7	A
8	figure it all out feel at home there soon
9	C
10	C
11	The student should explain that Deena had to change schools because her family moved to a new suburb and her old school was too far away to travel to each day.
12	The student should relate how Deena leaves school looking confident and happy to how she wants to please her father and not make him worry about her.
13	The student should list how Deena introduces herself, shows the new student around, and asks the new student to sit with her.
14	The student should describe how Deena's father says he is pleased and tells her she is brave for accepting all the changes and not letting her fear stop her.
15	The student should give a reasonable description of how Deena's experience of changing schools inspires her to help others. The answer should refer to how she understands how difficult it can be when starting a new school and how she decides it is important to make an effort to welcome new students.

Practice Set 13
Waste Not, Want Not

Question	Answer
1	B
2	D
3	B
4	The student may list how Ben took his parcel to the table, examined the knot before untying it, or untied the knot instead of cutting the string.
5	C
6	A
7	B
8	kindness
9	C
10	D
11	The student should describe how John's words show that he does not care about the whipcord. The answer may refer to how he asks what is so important about it, how he calls it "a bit of thread," how he says you can get whipcord for just three cents, or how he says that he does not care about three cents.
12	The student should explain how the tops need strings and how Ben is able to use the whipcord he kept for his string, while John does not have whipcord to use as a string.
13	The student should list the two actions below for happiness and the two actions below for unhappiness. Happiness: clapped his hands, danced for joy Unhappiness: frowned, crossed his arms
14	The student should give a reasonable explanation of what the last line shows about how John has changed. The answer may refer to how John now understands how useful whipcord is, now wishes he had kept his own whipcord, or now understands that he shouldn't be wasteful.
15	The student should give a reasonable explanation of what the play teaches about appreciating things and use relevant supporting details. The answer should refer to how Ben appreciates the whipcord, keeps it, and then finds it very useful. The answer should refer to how John does not appreciate the whipcord, does not keep it, and then wishes that he had.

Practice Set 14
The Grasshopper and the Ant

Question	Answer
1	B
2	Not a morsel or crumb in his cupboard –
3	A
4	A
5	D
6	C
7	D
8	The student should describe how the illustration shows the grasshopper singing and having fun while the ants work hard collecting food.
9	The student should explain that the grasshopper goes hungry in winter because he did not take action and collect food during summer.
10	The student should give a reasonable explanation as to why the ant chooses not to help the grasshopper. The student may infer that the ant thinks it is the grasshopper's own fault or thinks the grasshopper should work for his food like the ants did.

Practice Set 14
When Father Carves the Duck

Question	Answer
1	B
2	A
3	The student should complete the diagram with the four items below. potatoes, squash, cabbage, gravy
4	A
5	D
6	C
7	A
8	The student should list two details that shows that the poem is meant to be humorous. The answer may refer to how the family members try to hide, how the food flies around and goes everywhere, how the family members get gravy on their faces, or how the family members walk around picking up duck from the window-sills and walls.
9	The student should complete the table with the words and phrases below. chips of duck – flying platter – slip dishes – skip potatoes – fly amuck squash and cabbage – leap in space
10	The student should describe how the poem suggests that the family members are amused. The answer may refer to how the family members prepare for the food to go flying or how the mother laughs at the father in the last stanza.

Practice Set 15
Cinderella

Question	Answer
1	B
2	B
3	B
4	The student may list how the sisters dance into the house, clap their hands, twirl each other around, or sing that they have been invited to the king's ball.
5	A
6	C
7	B
8	The student should complete the diagram with the details below. coach, two horses, coachman, footman
9	D
10	B
11	The student should describe how the fairy godmother uses magic to make Cinderella a coach, horses, and two men to take her to the ball, and how she uses magic to make her a dress and shoes to wear.
12	The student should explain that the prince uses the slipper to find Cinderella. The answer should refer to how he searches for the person who the slipper fits and how he knows that this is the person he will marry.
13	The student may list how the prince says he will only marry the person who owns the slipper, how the prince "hunted far and wide," or how hundreds of people tried on the slipper to see if it would fit.
14	The student should make a reasonable inference about how the older sisters feel when the slipper fits Cinderella. The student may infer that they are surprised, shocked, confused, or jealous. The answer should be supported with a reasonable explanation.
15	The student should explain how the story "Cinderella" has a happy ending and use relevant supporting details. The answer may refer to how sad Cinderella is at the start of the passage, how hard she has to work and how poorly she is treated, how she meets a prince and marries him, or how the prince saves her from her hard life and they live happily ever after.

Practice Set 16
Betty's Reward

Question	Answer
1	cook
2	The student should describe how Washington asks Betty to make breakfast and how her cooking skills allow her to cook breakfast for him.
3	The student should list how there is going to be a parade and how someone is making a welcome speech.
4	D
5	The student should complete the table with the details below. Robert – hardly eats any breakfast Mother – forgets to put coffee in the coffee pot Father – keeps checking his watch
6	A
7	B
8	A
9	The student may list how Betty curtsies, calls the man "sir," agrees to make breakfast, sets the table with the best cloth and silver, or invites the strangers in for breakfast.
10	The student should complete the web with the items below. bread, honey, butter, milk, eggs, ham
11	C
12	C
13	The student should explain that the coach arriving is the same as the one Betty described as being Washington's coach.
14	The student may infer that Betty was proud of herself, excited to have met and cooked for Washington, or amazed by the events. The student should refer to how she told the story everyone she knew and to her children, which suggests that the events were special to her or meant a lot to her.
15	The student should describe two good deeds that Betty does and how she is rewarded for them. The answer should use relevant supporting details. The good deeds listed should be that she agreed to stay home so everyone else could see Washington, and how she agreed to make the strangers breakfast. The answer should describe how her reward is meeting Washington and having him kiss her on the cheek.

Made in the USA
Las Vegas, NV
11 March 2022

45443783R00103